The Only Freedom

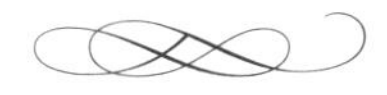

The Only Freedom

Joel S. Goldsmith

Edited by
Lorraine Sinkler

Acropolis Books, Publisher
Atlanta, Georgia

Published by Acropolis Books

Printed in the United States of America

For information contact:
ACROPOLIS BOOKS, INC.
Atlanta, Georgia

www.acropolisbooks.com

Cover and text design: Tonya Beach Creative Services

Library of Congress Cataloging-in-Publication Data

Goldsmith, Joel S., 1892-1964.

The only freedom / Joel S. Goldsmith ; edited by Lorraine Sinkler.
p. cm.
Includes bibliographical references.
ISBN 1-889051-70-5 (alk. paper)
1. Spiritual life. I. Sinkler, Lorraine. II. Title.
BP610.G641597 2006
299'.93--dc22

2005023992

Except the Lord build the house,
they labour in vain that build it. . .
– Psalm 127

"Illumination dissolves all material ties and binds men together with the golden chains of spiritual understanding; it acknowledges only the leadership of the Christ; it has no ritual or rule but the divine, impersonal universal Love; no other worship than the inner Flame that is ever lit at the shrine of Spirit. This union is the free state of spiritual brotherhood. The only restraint is the discipline of Soul; therefore, we know liberty without license; we are a united universe without physical limits, a divine service to God without ceremony or creed. The illumined walk without fear – by Grace."

–*The Infinite Way* by Joel S. Goldsmith

Dedication

Twentieth century mystic Joel S. Goldsmith revealed to the Western world the nature and substance of mystical living that demonstrated how mankind can live in the consciousness of God. The clarity and insight of his teachings, called the Infinite Way, were captured in more than thirty-five books and in over twelve hundred hours of tape recordings that, today, perpetuate his message.

Joel faithfully arranged to have prepared from his class tapes, monthly letters which were made available as one of the most important tools to assist students in their study and application of the Infinite Way teachings. He felt each of these letters came from an ever-new insight that would produce a deeper level of understanding and awareness of truth as students worked diligently with this fresh and timely material.

Each yearly compilation of the *Letters* focused on a central theme, and it became apparent that working with an entire year's material built an ascending level of consciousness. The *Letters* were subsequently published as books, each containing all the year's letters. The publications became immensely popular as they proved to be of great assistance in the individual student's development of spiritual awareness.

Starting in 1954, the monthly letters were made availiable to students wishing to subscribe to them. Each year of the *Letters* was published individually during 1954 through 1959 and made available in book form. From 1960 through 1970 the *Letters* were published and renamed as books with the titles:

1960 Letters	*Our Spiritual Resources*
1961 Letters	*The Contemplative Life*
1962 Letters	*Man Was Not Born to Cry*
1963 Letters	*Living Now*
1964 Letters	*Realization of Oneness*
1965 Letters	*Beyond Words and Thoughts*
1966 Letters	*The Mystical I*
1967 Letters	*Living Between Two Worlds*
1968 Letters	*The Altitude of Prayer*
1969 Letters	*Consciousness Is What I Am*
1970 Letters	*Awakening Mystical Consciousness*

Joel worked closely with his editor, Lorraine Sinkler, to ensure each letter carried the continuity, integrity, and pure consciousness of the message. After Joel's transition in 1964, Emma A. Goldsmith (Joel's wife) requested that Lorraine continue working with the monthly letters, drawing as in the past from the inexhaustible tape recordings of his class work with students. The invaluable work by Lorraine and Emma has ensured that this message will be preserved and available in written form for future generations. Acropolis Books is honored and privileged to offer in book form the next eleven years of Joel's teaching.

The 1971 through 1981 *Letters* also carry a central theme for each year, and have been renamed with the following titles:

1971 Letters	*Living by the Word*
1972 Letters	*Living the Illumined Life*
1973 Letters	*Seek Ye First*
1974 Letters	*Spiritual Discernment: the Healing Consciousness*
1975 Letters	*A Message for the Ages*
1976 Letters	*I Stand on Holy Ground*
1977 Letters	*The Art of Spiritual Living*
1978 Letters	*God Formed Us for His Glory*
1979 Letters	*The Journey Back to the Father's House*
1980 Letters	*Showing Forth the Presence of God*
1981 Letters	*The Only Freedom*

Acropolis Books dedicates this series of eleven books to Lorraine Sinkler and Emma A. Goldsmith for their ongoing commitment to ensure that these teachings will never be lost to the world.

Table of Contents

Chapter One

A Message for the New Year

This is the time of year when you wish all those with whom you come in contact a happy New Year. You should realize that in doing this you are not benefiting those to whom you wish this happy New Year, nor are you doing anything to bring them a happy New Year by your wishing them one. Under certain conditions, however, you, yourself, are benefiting by wishing other people a happy New Year, but you must know what those certain conditions are. No one can bring a happy or prosperous New Year to another or a joyous one. Only the individual can do that for himself.

Determining Factors in Achieving a Happy New Year

You can wish a person a happy New Year but it will do nothing for him. The only thing that will ensure a happy New Year for him is whether or not he is living in accord with loving the Lord, his God, with all his soul, all his heart, and all his mind, and loving his neighbor as himself. To the extent of his violation of that he cannot have the happy New Year that you might wish him and would like for him to have. You cannot give it to anyone. Only he, himself, can determine the degree of the happiness of the New Year, and he determines that by the degree of his loving God and his neighbor as himself. Those are the determining factors in whether or not he will have a happy New Year.

But this must not stop you from wishing a person a happy New Year because in the degree that you are wishing for others a happy New Year, in that degree are you loving your neighbor as yourself, in that degree are you loving God, and in that degree are you fulfilling the terms that will ensure you, yourself, a happy and prosperous New Year. But there is one catch to it and this is the one for which you must watch.

Embrace All Mankind in Your Good Wishes

When you wish a person a happy New Year, be sure that in your mind you are not wishing him personally a happy New Year, but that you are including all mankind, recognizing that every person is a branch of the one tree and, therefore, what you wish for one you must wish for all, or you, yourself, have nothing. Try to wish good for one branch of the tree and forget the other branches and see what effect it would have. None. Unless your love and your wishes are embracing every branch of the tree, you are wasting your breath, because you are accepting a selfhood apart from God; or it may be that in back of your mind you are actually believing that God can bless one without blessing another, and this is not possible for God's love is universal. "God is no respecter of persons,"[1] or of races or religions. To God we are all one.

Mankind does not benefit simply because you include it because it is excluding itself. But for your own sake, you must include all men whether or not they reject the good wishes you offer. Whether or not they reject the love you offer is not your concern. Your concern is never to forget the tree of Life. Never forget that God made man in his image and likeness, meaning all men. You love the Lord, your God, by knowing that God is universal, impersonal, impartial. By including all mankind, you are loving your neighbor as yourself and therefore, you are fulfilling the Two Commandments, and obedience to these Two Commandments constitutes the harmony of your being. Not only are you one with the tree and the tree one with the entire earth, grounded in God, but all men—friends or foes—are also branches of the tree, the same tree, one with the source.

When you are praying, you cannot possibly believe that you can bring God to a person for God is already there. Your prayer is merely the conscious remembrance of Omnipresence. You do not bring God to anyone; you do not bring anyone to God: you bring to conscious remembrance the omnipresence, omnipotence, and omniscience of God. Unless you are including all mankind, you are omitting yourself and probably your relative's, neighbor's, or patient's self.

The Universal Nature of the Fatherhood of God

To love God with all your heart is not an emotional experience. It is an acknowledgment of God as your Father and as the Father of the friend and the Father of the enemy. It is obeying the Master's precept, "Call no man your father upon the earth: for one is your Father, which is in heaven."[2] This is your Father, my Father, his Father, her Father, your friend's Father, and your enemies' Father.

You love God only when you acknowledge the universal nature of the fatherhood of God, the universal nature of the power and presence of God. And, unless you can see God as the God of all, of all those who were, all those who are, and all those who are to be, you are not loving God supremely. Then, unless you can see every individual as equally one with God, the child of God, the offspring of God, under God's jurisdiction, you are not loving your neighbor as yourself.

Why Some Persons Are Not Benefited by Your Recognition of Spiritual Identity

You can know the truth about the universal nature of God and the universal nature of man in God's image and likeness, and yet not everyone will be benefited by your knowing that truth, even though you are knowing it equally for all. The reason is that if a person holds himself outside the love of God and love of man, then it is he who is withholding himself from God, not God who is withholding Itself from him.

The truth that you know about God and man is what sets man free from universal beliefs, from the sense of separation from God. All men should benefit equally by that truth. Those who do not benefit are those who withhold themselves from this universal truth. They do not make themselves a part of it; they do not include themselves in it; they do not realize that every time you say, "Happy New Year," within your mind you are addressing this to man universally. Every time you wish "Godspeed" to one, every time you say "Aloha" to one, within yourself you must be addressing universal man, the Christ-man, the spiritual man, the child of God eternally everywhere. This is the nature of prayer in spiritual work.

Recognize Universal Christhood

In mental treatments, you can address a treatment to Jones, Brown, or Smith, or to your particular dog or cat and bring some measure of benefit to any of these because it is all done by mental impartation from one mind to another. But in the spiritual life, you bring the grace of God into your experience and through you into the experience of others only in proportion as you recognize universal Christhood.

Christhood is the divine and true nature of individual man, and this has been the truth since God began. Christhood did not begin two thousand years ago: It began in the beginning with God, for man has coexisted with God since the beginning of time; therefore, man has been the Christ since the beginning of time. Jesus merely called attention to the Christhood that existed before Abraham was, that is, before the days of what anyone knew as the first religion. In a mystical writing it is said, "Before God"—meaning before any man had any concept of God—*"I* existed as individual being and entity." I and my Father in our oneness have coexisted in that oneness as long as God has been, and that is eternally.

This is our assurance that immortality is, for that which has had no beginning can have no ending. The relationship that I have had with my Father since the beginning is our eternal relationship as long as God lasts. And God is infinite, eternal, immortal being. Therefore I am infinite, eternal, immortal being, as are you. It is our recognition of this that constitutes our immortality and enables us to say with Paul, "Neither death nor life. . . shall be able to separate us from the love of God," the life of God. Neither life nor death can separate you from God, for your relationship with God is eternal.

Have You Accepted the Fatherhood of God and the Brotherhood of Man as Universally Applicable?

The Christ has coexisted with God since the beginning. It is your recognition of this universal Fatherhood of God and brotherhood of man that enables you to ensure for yourself a happy and prosperous New Year and enables your wish for a happy New Year for others to be fruitful in their experience. It cannot be fruitful just to wish one individual a happy New Year because in doing that you have set up a branch separate and apart from God. When you say, "Happy New Year," and have in your mind's eye the tree of Life and include all the branches, then your wish for other's happiness in the new year will bear fruit in the lives of all those who can accept the Fatherhood of God and the brotherhood of man. It makes no difference whether the acknowledgment comes through a spiritual teaching, a church teaching, or the teaching of a fraternal order. What counts is whether or not you are saying it from the heart, whether you in your heart have accepted the universal Fatherhood of God and the universal brotherhood of man, and whether you love the Lord your God in this way and your neighbor as yourself by including all neighbors.

Address All Consciousness Universally

When Jesus Christ said, "My peace I give unto you," it would seem that he was addressing only his disciples or those gathered to hear him speak, but he said elsewhere, "My words shall not pass away."[5] When you say, "My peace I give unto you," you are addressing the son of God: those who have been; those who are now; and those who are to be. Your assurance of a spiritually fruitful New Year depends on your ability consciously throughout the year—not only on New Year's Day, but throughout the year—to remember this lesson, to remember daily to breathe out to the world, "My peace give I unto you. The Christ-peace do I give."

Addressing this message of peace to all consciousness universally, it returns to you as part of that consciousness, but it also touches the consciousness of all who are attuned to the love of God and the love of neighbor. If it does not reach all mankind, it is because there are still some having a personal God of their own or including as their neighbor only those they desire to include. By this they withhold from themselves the blessing you would bring to them. For you to make yourself a part of what we call the Infinite Way consciousness, it is necessary that you open yourself each day to extending a "Happy New Year; peace on earth as it is in heaven" unto all. Thereby good returns unto you and at the same time blesses the world.

Invite the World Into a Relationship of Universal Brotherhood

The world is your individual responsibility as much as your family or your community is. If you can believe that Lao Tzu, Buddha, or Jesus included the entire universe in their ministry and that they were declaring universal truths about all mankind, you will understand that they accepted the responsibility for revealing Christhood or Buddhahood universally.

As the Christ, one with God, it is as much your responsibility to travel this world and bless it as it is the responsibility of any spiritual teacher, for such teachers have been given no responsibility that is not given to you. It is not necessary, however, to leave home to travel the world and bless mankind. That is just a temporary function of some individuals. But it in no way relieves you of the responsibility of opening your soul-consciousness every day and traveling this world, inviting into universal brotherhood, divine brotherhood, spiritual sonship, all men and all mankind, and at the same time forgiving them their sins.

Christhood was revealed to the world in one of the highest manifestations in the man Christ Jesus. He was the way-shower, showing you the way in which you must go to follow in his footsteps and acknowledge the Christ. Acknowledge your Christhood, but acknowledge it without any sense of egotism. Egotism would deprive anyone of this divine relationship with God.

Every Day, the Beginning of a New Year

Just as you have learned in spiritual work that Sunday is seven days a week and that you must not only live seven days a week as you are taught to live on Sunday, the sabbath, but that there must be no difference in your conduct, in your thought, in your consciousness, or in your life on any of the seven days of the week, so you will learn that it is not only January first that is New Year's Day, but that a new year actually begins every day of the week.

Therefore, if you are not living in the consciousness of "Happy New Year, *My* peace I give unto thee, God's grace is with thee," every day throughout the year, then you are setting aside only one day as New Year's Day and this is valueless, because every second of every minute of every hour actually marks the beginning of a new year.

Live Now, Second by Second, and Wipe Out the Past

Every second is the beginning of a new life because in any second and in every second you can wipe out your past. You do not have to wait for the first day of January to begin a new life. You do not have to wait for January first to forgive or to be forgiven. You do not have to wait for January first to wish the whole world peace on earth. You do not have to wait for January first to stop hating or to eliminate prejudice, bias, and bigotry from consciousness. You can begin a new life in any second. But you can also bring to others a new life in any second of their experience by opening the door of consciousness in this way and admitting them to divine grace.

Evidence of the Activity of the Christ in Human Consciousness

You are witnessing a greater change in human consciousness in recent times, carrying the world spiritually forward, that has been taking place in the past hundred years. It is the fruitage of the change that is taking place in human consciousness. The past one hundred years or more of metaphysical, spiritual, and the beginning of mystical teaching in this age are changing human consciousness, bringing about such changes that every year you can see tremendous progress in the minds of men.

A change has taken place in the attitude and care of the mentally disturbed and in the handling of the aged poor, showing the change that has taken place universally in human consciousness. There must be a reason for it. Human consciousness must be opening itself to this change, and then there must be more of the Christ manifest in human consciousness to bring it about. All of this dates only from the metaphysical work which had its beginning in this age, and it will keep on increasing as metaphysical and spiritual work continues to abound throughout the world.

You will also witness the breaking up of error in what looks to be warfare and persecution. There is no way for the transition to take place except through the breaking up of human consciousness. In proportion as we try to hold on to the *status quo,* as we try to hold on to yesterday's manna, to yesterday, and to the past, warfare and large and small conflicts on earth will continue. But you are privileged to witness the world-wide breaking up of man's inhumanity to man, of man's holding other men in bondage. You are witnessing the activity of the Christ in human consciousness.

Purifying Consciousness

What is bringing about this change in human consciousness? What is bringing about a change in your individual consciousness and mine? It is the actual realization of the Presence. It is not talk about It; It is not sermons about It or books about It: it is the experience of the realized Christ that does it. The purpose of spiritual talks, lectures, or books is to help you bring about a purification of your own consciousness so that the Christ may enter and be consciously recognized.

Without purification the Christ does not enter. The natural man or the human being does not receive the Christ of God. It is only when the natural man begins to purify his consciousness and brings about a transition within himself that the Christ can find entrance. Through the Infinite Way, you have a certain principle to put into practice to aid in this process. What have you in your house? This is the question to which you address yourself: What have I in my house or in my consciousness that I can give, that I can forgive, that I can bestow, that I can share? What have I in my consciousness?

As you begin to let the spirit of God, the grace of God, flow through you to this world individually and collectively, as you permit yourself to be an outlet for God's grace, in that proportion are you purifying your consciousness and making the soil ready for the conception and birth of the Christ in you.

Become Alive to the Christ in You

It is only when you become alive to the Christ in you that the Christ is active on earth through you. In your preparatory state, the Christ is not released on earth through you. Only when you finally come to the actual experience of feeling the Presence within you, hearing the voice within you, or recognizing something other than yourself and higher than yourself within you, only from that moment on are you releasing the Christ into this world because only at that moment is Christ alive and active in you.

Only after a certain moment could Paul say, "I live; yet not I, but Christ liveth in me."[6] Only after a certain moment could Jesus say, "The Spirit of the Lord is upon me, because he hath anointed me to preach the gospel to the poor; he hath sent me to heal the broken hearted, to preach deliverance to the captives, and recovering of sight to the blind, to set at liberty them that are bruised."[7] "The Father that dwelleth in me, he doeth the works."[8] He could say that only when the Father had come alive in him. Up to the moment when the Father comes alive in you, the Christ is a potentiality in you or dormant in you, but you prepare yourself for the birth of the Christ in you by these spiritual works that you are reading and accepting, by the spiritual truth you meditate upon, ponder, and then eventually put into practice. "What have I in the house?" Then begin to loose "the imprisoned splendor," and from that moment on the Christ is released in you and begins to function in human consciousness, changing the entire nature of human consciousness.

Those in metaphysical movements or out of them who are students of spiritual wisdom would be healers if the Christ were awake in them, because they read many of the same books and they have the same truth; and therefore the fruitage should be the same. But it is not. These books, these teachings, these teachers are all there for the purpose of awakening them to the Christ, of bringing to life the Christ in them, so that at some particular moment of their life they can say, "The spirit of God is upon me. The Christ is awake within me."

When the moment comes, be assured that you will never say it orally, nor will you ever breathe it to another soul. It will be made manifest by its fruits, not by words, not by speech—by its fruits. It will never be necessary for you to announce it any more than it was ever necessary for Jesus to announce that he was the Christ.

From Being a Branch to Being the Tree

Live in the consciousness of the tree of Life. Make the fifteenth chapter of John a part of your very flesh, blood, and bone, so that you live day by day in the consciousness of your Christhood. At the moment you may see yourself as the branch of the tree, but in that day when the Christ announces Itself in you, your position in life changes, and you are no longer the branch of the tree: you are the tree, one with God.

When the Christ lives in you, you are the tree. You are the divine Son of God consciously born, made manifest. "I live; yet not I, but Christ liveth in me." There is now no "man, whose breath is in his nostrils"[9]: there is only spiritual Sonship, and this divine Sonship is the light of the world. This is your identity when the spark is ignited within you, when the spirit of the Lord God is upon you. It is then that you have attained

Buddhahood, or Christhood.

In all mystical teachings, Buddhahood or Christhood is your true identity, and it is possible of attainment here on earth. It is your identity the moment the Christ announces Itself within you, whether you hear the voice or whether you have the feeling. Regardless of how the Christ announces Itself, you will know by the fruitage in your life, by your change of base, by the fact that you are no longer a receiver: you are a giver. You are the instrument of God's giving, a transparency through which God appears as harmony on earth.

When Christhood is attained, It performs that which is given you to do. It is the Presence that goes before you to "make the crooked places straight."[10] It is that which heals, forgives, multiplies loaves and fishes, and It is possible of attainment here and now. The way the Master gave us was by obedience to the two great Commandments. As you come to know the nature of God and the nature of spiritual man, you are loving God and you are loving your neighbor as yourself. You must overcome all your former beliefs about God until you come to know Him aright, for only this is life eternal.

As you have made every day of the week your Sabbath, so make every day of the year your New Year, and through this recognition of the Fatherhood of God and the brotherhood of man be the instrument through which God's grace reaches human consciousness every day, all day, all night.

Instead of the words, "Happy New Year," use the Master's words, "*My* grace, *My* peace, give I unto thee."

Tape Recorded Excerpts
Prepared by the Editor

In this month's letter, Joel points out that the New Year begins not only on the first day of January of every year, but that every day, in fact, every moment of every day is the beginning of a New Year. How important, then, it is to go within at the beginning of each new day and be securely anchored in omnipresence, omniscience, and omnipotence.

The excerpts below will help you to begin each day with confidence and assurance, knowing that you do not walk alone.

How to Begin the New Day

"Evil of any and every nature operates invisibly as a belief in two powers and, because this is a universal belief, it acts universally in human consciousness. To the degree that we do not consciously reject it, we become victims of it. Therefore, it is necessary that we start every day with a form of realization which, in my writings, we have called protective work.

"Protective work is probably the most important part of all the work in the Infinite Way. The reason is that if you have sufficiently protected yourself, you will have that much less need of overcoming anything because you will avoid those things that ordinarily we have to overcome. Protective work is not a protection *from* anything or *from* anybody. It is not protective work in that sense. It is protective work in the sense of protecting ourselves from the operation of universal belief. You will need constant reminders of it for at least a year, daily reminders of it, until it has become so deeply rooted and grounded in you to do this protective work that it becomes automatic and is done without conscious thinking.

"Whatever sins or diseases, lacks, limitations, storms, wars, infections, or contagions that take place throughout this day are actually the operation of universal belief, the carnal mind, the veil of illusion. Since this universal belief of a selfhood apart from God, of a power apart from God is not God-ordained, this belief has no person in whom, on whom, or through whom to operate. It has no power, and it has no law. As a matter of fact, it is not an *it.* It is an illusion. It is merely a belief that derives its seeming power by acceptance, and I hereby reject it. I consciously reject the belief that there is any power but that of God, Spirit. I consciously reject the belief that there is a material or mental law with power, since God is Spirit, and God is the only law and lawgiver. Therefore all law must be spiritual.

"Since everything that operates has to operate as law, you have nullified everything but the spiritual law of God, the law of good, the law of harmony, the law of justice, equity, equality, the law of peace, the law of dominion. . . . Choose, when you awaken in the morning, whether you are going to allow yourself to serve the universal belief in two powers or whether you are going to be God-governed. You can be God-governed. You can be God-governed only by an act of your own consciousness because without this, you, just like every other human being in the world, are subject unto the powers that be, the so-called powers of carnal mind. You must come out and be separate. You must bring yourself out from under the universal belief in two powers and establish yourself in the grace of God, and realize that there are no powers to operate in, on, or through you, or on anyone except God's grace, for I and the Father are one."

Joel S. Goldsmith, "Protective Work".
The 1960 Denver Closed Class. Tape 1:1.

"In living the Infinite Way, then, you are doing two things all day long. You are doing protective work and you are doing treatment or healing work. You are engaged in those two activities all day long whether or not anybody asks you for help. . . . From the moment of your waking in the morning, you are doing protective work. Do not think of protective work in the sense of protecting yourself from evil or anything else. Protective work is the realization that there is no power from which to protect oneself. . . . Protective work is living in the realization that since there is only one power, there are no other powers to do anything or to be anything, and any suggestion of such is this mesmeric influence or mortal mind, or 'arm of flesh', or nothingness.

"Without this, even if you are not consciously thinking of accidents or discords, diseases, sins, or temptations, you are permitting yourself to accept unconsciously or subconsciously the world's mesmerism, the world's hypnotic suggestions. In other words, evil touches our lives in very much the same way as subliminal perception operates. . . It enters in the form of suggestions or mental impositions. . . Unless there is a realization that it isn't power, that it is not an emanation of God, it can take root in you and appear in any form or every form. . . .

"In this early part of our conscious activity it is necessary that often throughout the day when we receive suggestions of accident, sickness, sin, war, depression, lack, or unemployment, as soon as these things touch our consciousness, we be alert enough to know that this is the tempter, this is the temptation, this is a suggestion from that universal mind of a power and presence apart from God, and then reject it in the realization that this is nothing but the fleshly mind or 'arm of flesh'; this is not power; this is not God-ordained; this has no law of God behind it. Then you are through with it. It takes a minute, but you have consciously set up within yourself the power of truth, and truth being infinite, nothing else can enter."

Joel S. Goldsmith. "Three Principles and Their Practice, *The 1959 Hawaiian Village Closed Class.* Tape 2:2.

"Because of omnipresence, can I ever be outside the presence of God? No, if I go up to heaven, He is there; if I go down to hell, He is there, and if I walk through the 'valley of the shadow of death', He is there. This is the meaning of omnipresence: I am never outside the presence of God, and it makes no difference if I am in a bar room or any other place, I am never outside the presence of God.

"But what does that mean? . . . It means that the God that is omnipresent is also all-wise, all-wisdom, and, therefore, knows my need before I do, making it unnecessary for me to pray for anything. Since here where I am, and it makes no difference if it is up in an airplane, down in a submarine, or on the battle front, here where I am is omnipresence, and the nature of omnipresence is omniscience, all knowing, all-wisdom.

"Then finally, this omnipresence which is the all-wisdom is omnipotence or all-power. So where I am, there are no other powers. Here is the secret of freeing ourselves from the discords of earth and maintaining that freedom: the conscious recognition of omnipresence, omniscience, and omnipotence which is only one power. Therefore, do I have to turn to God for healing or for protection? No, for the omnipresence of God is the all-wisdom and the all-power besides which there is no other power. I cannot need protection from the power of God, and there is no other power if omnipotence is omnipotent."

Joel S. Goldsmith. "The Need for Religion in Our Lives,"
The 1963 Instructions for Teaching the Infinite Way. Tape 6:2.

Chapter Two

Neither Do I Condemn Thee

Behold, thou art made whole: sin no more,
lest a worse thing come unto thee.
John 5:14

Neither do I condemn thee: go, and sin no more.
John 8:11

The Master's words to the woman taken in adultery, to the thief on the cross, and to the man born blind were all in the same vein: "Neither do I condemn thee." Always he saw only spiritual being. Yet even though he saw these so-called sinners and apparently diseased persons as spiritual beings, he had the wisdom to know that they had not been seeing themselves spiritually, and so he added, "I have taken the burden away from you, but go and sin no more, lest a worse thing come upon you." In other words, "I have seen you spiritually; I have set you free; but what are you going to do about that freedom tomorrow?"

"Whatsoever a man soweth, that shall he also reap. For he that soweth to the flesh shall of the flesh reap corruption; but he that soweth to the Spirit shall of the Spirit reap life everlasting."[1] And what does it mean to sow to the flesh except to have fleshly ideas of man? If we look upon man as either good or bad, rich or poor, sick or well, we are sowing to the flesh, but if we hold man in consciousness as eternal, immortal, spiritual being, we are sowing to the Spirit. We do the sowing and we also do the reaping. Every time we behold anyone as less than the Christ, in that degree will it react upon us.

One Self

There is only one Self—Self spelled with a capital "S." That Self is God, the one Being, the one Life, the one Mind, the one Soul. That one Self is infinitely expressing Itself as children of God, as offspring of the One. If we had a fixture with a dozen electric light bulbs on it, there would still be only one electricity flowing through each bulb, and the power in each bulb would be of the same nature and quality as its substance, electricity. That would be true if there were a million bulbs. The electricity manifested or expressed in each bulb would be the same one electricity.

So the life that is expressed in any home or community by two or three persons, or by two or three million persons is the one Life and the one Intelligence. Just as the different sized electric light bulbs draw forth different amounts of electricity, even though it is still the one electricity, so we show forth varying degrees of that one Life. That same one Life is in the flowers, in the animals, vegetables, and minerals—one Consciousness, one Intelligence; there is only one Soul, one Spirit, and there is only one Selfhood. Anything that we do is done within that Selfhood, although apparently we do it to another or for another.

The soul of every individual on earth is the soul of God. That brings us to the great truth that whenever we do anything of a good nature to anyone, we are not doing it to or for someone else: we are doing it to or for our Self because that Self is our being as well as his. The same principle applies when something of an erroneous nature is done to you: it is not done to you because there is no you separate and apart from any other person. "Is there a God beside me?" asks Isaiah. "Yea, there is no God; I know not any."[2] God is the only "me"; and that "me" is the only God. God is the activity of our being. God is the soul of our being. Is there any other? That one is you; that one is I. There is only one.

What We Do to Others We Do to Ourselves

Is it surprising that in the recognition of that oneness the Master revealed that we are not to do our benevolences publicly, to be seen of men, or in order to get credit for them? He knew that what we are doing is not for the sake of the other fellow, but for our own self. Why, then, should we seek credit for doing something which redounds to the glory of our own self? On the other hand, the very moment that we do evil to another, let us never forget that the evil is done to our self. It is not necessary for any man to find out what we have done in order for us to be punished. The punishment comes from within ourselves because, by setting up a selfhood apart from that one Self, we have set up a conflict within us. The moment we think we have done or could do harm to another, we have set up a selfhood apart from God. If we could accept the revelation that there is but one Self, knowing that what we do is to ourself, would it then be possible for us to do injury to anyone?

Where Is the Responsibility for Good or Evil in Our Experience?

At this stage of our unfoldment, we must understand why neither credit nor blame should attach itself to us or to another. The credit belongs to the impulse which brought forth the good deed; the discredit belongs to the ignorance of this great truth of the one Self. It is only our ignorance of this truth that would permit us to do a misdeed, not that the punishment is any less because we did it ignorantly. The punishment will follow but an understanding of the way this operates will prevent us from indulging in condemnation—either self-condemnation or condemnation of another.

How can we blame someone else for our failure if there is only one Self? Almost everybody who fails is sure that his failure lies at somebody else's door. It is always some other person's fault, and if not some other person, then some national, racial, or religious group, or if nothing else it is the government's fault; but always somebody else is to blame for the terrible plight in which some persons find themselves. They seldom are willing to take the blame for it.

We are free the moment we realize: "No one has ever injured me. No one ever had the power to injure me. Whatever has been done, I did to myself. I may have done it ignorantly, not realizing what I was doing, but with this knowledge, I know that it was I who brought it about in my own experience and nobody else. Any blame that I place at the other person's feet is hiding from the truth. I have created good in my life and I have created evil in my life. I have benefited by the good and I have suffered from the evil, but no one else has done anything to me that I myself did not empower him to do.

"I create the good in my life and I create the evil in my life because the moment I deviate in my thought of you or conduct toward you as if you were other than the one Self, then am I bringing upon me the penalty which comes from entertaining such ignorance. For me to believe that there is a you separate and apart from me, separate and apart from the one Self, will tempt me to think something other of you than I really know about myself. Furthermore, unless I see that God constitutes individual being, I shall ultimately be led through that ignorance to act in some way to you as if you were other than myself, again bringing the penalty upon my shoulders. If I ascribe to you any quality, character, or characteristic which is not a part of the Godhead, I am thereby declaring a selfhood apart from God and setting up my own punishment."

Anything of which we are ignorant ultimately brings us punishment. So if we are ignorant of the one Self, ultimately we must pay the penalty for that ignorance. Never doubt that the good we do is done unto ourselves, and the only reward is in the doing. There is no reward from outside. The evil that we do is an evil against ourselves and results in the opposite of reward—punishment; but this also comes from within ourselves. Even if "man, whose breath is in his nostrils"[3] never discovers the evil deed, never brings us into court, never imprisons us, that which we are in secret knows what we are and it rewards us openly or punishes us openly.

When Does Forgiveness Come?

The reason the world rises in rebellion against the teaching of the one Self is that it makes every person amenable to himself; it makes him responsible to himself and for himself. It does not permit him the luxury of mouthing such platitudes as, "Oh, God will forgive us our sins." Nonsense! God never forgives our sins any more than God punishes our sins. The punishment for our sin lasts just as long as the sin lasts, because whatever is done, we do it to ourselves.

We can forgive each other if we happen to be sufficiently good-natured or loving, but that does not exempt us from the punishment for our misdemeanors. No, regardless of how much we may forgive each other, there is no forgiveness. The only forgiveness is in returning to our Father's house, to our principle, and again living in harmony with that principle. It is pure fiction to believe in some God in heaven who is going to look down and forgive us while we are out marauding. True, we can confess our sins and be forgiven instantly, but what about an hour from now when the sin begins all over again? The Master had a sharp answer for that: "lest a worse thing come unto thee."

He did not preach a God who permits us to go on our way sinning with impunity and then reassures us with a gentle, "I forgive you." No, his teaching was, "I forgive you; *go, and sin no more."* Do you believe the Master?

Every time we come to a place in our consciousness where we actually give up our errors of thought and deed, we are washed white as snow. Every time we confess, not necessarily outwardly, but inwardly, to our errors of omission or commission, and realize that it was an error and feel that deep sense of contrition in which we know it cannot happen again, we are made pure. We are never held in bondage to anything once we have recognized it as error and have forsaken it. Every time we come to a place of inner grief over our errors, we are forgiven. That ends the episode, but it carries with it the command, "Sin no more, lest a worse thing come unto thee." It makes us—not God—responsible for what we are thinking and for what we are doing.

Sometimes our own sins are not forgiven until we have forgiven our enemies. "Forgive us our trespasses as"—in proportion as—"we forgive those who trespass against us." Very often we are held in unforgiveness until we have found some way of forgiving, until we have released, pardoned, or ceased to hold resentment against those we may believe have wronged us. Whatever the enemy we are entertaining—political, national, international, religious, racial, or personal—we have to make our peace with him.

Looking Through the Good and the Evil

If, in our consciousness, we are holding somebody in bondage to being an evil human being or even a good human being, we have not made our peace with him. We must rise to that place in consciousness where not only are there no evil human beings but where there also are no good human beings. Everyone takes his rightful place as a child of God. We have not forgiven the trespasses of the world as long as we say, "You are a good human being or you are an evil human being." We understand the nature of forgiveness only when we are able to look through the good and the evil and realize, "Thou art the child of God in whom He is well pleased."

Making Peace with One Another

It matters not what our sins are outwardly. They represent the generations which have lived with a sense of separation from God. Our sins and our poverty and our diseases will continue, not because of God—God stands available—but they will continue until we have made our peace with our fellow man. The reason we have not understood this before, and been able to implement it in our lives is because we have believed in many selves, our own self and some other self, and so we have felt that something could be true of ourselves which was not true of our brother's self. Therefore, we have treated our brother differently from the way in which we treated ourself, all because of the belief of two selves. We lost our way because we have forgotten that the self which is doing the condemning or the praising is the same self which is being condemned or praised. Therein lies the entire mystery.

Would anybody in the world harm another physically, mentally, morally, or financially if he really knew that he was doing it to himself? The Master told us that God is your Father and God is my Father, therefore, we be brethren, not separate persons, but members of one household. If we harm one person in the household, we harm the whole household, because a household is not a separate thing made up of component parts. A household is one entity, made up of love, and when in any way we violate love in that household, we have violated the household. And that household we are. We are the city of God, divine consciousness, the one household of God, the one universal being, the temple of the living God.

Only the person who can live as unto the Self can rise above karmic law into grace, but karmic law is only a way station. When we have brought ourselves into obedience to karmic law so that we recognize only the one Self, we are then under grace. The moment we have annihilated all sense of a selfhood apart from God, we are under grace. We are no more under law, not even karmic law, because now we are not doing anything to another. Now we have no other Self to whom to do good. Only in that place in consciousness do we rise above karmic law—in that moment when we have no self to bless or to condemn. When we have no other self than the one Self, we are under grace.

There is no way of excusing ourselves for our faults, but that does not mean that we hold ourselves in constant condemnation. Some of our faults may be with us for a long time to come, but we should learn to forgive ourselves quickly; we should pick ourselves up more easily and try to see that there is no repetition of the same mistake. Each day will be a day of atonement and a day for us to begin again with a steadfast resolve, remembering Jesus' injunction, "Go, and sin no more."

A New Concept of Sin

This is a new concept of what constitutes sin: we are learning now that when we say that anyone is good or evil, young or old, well or sick, we are thereby sinning. We now recognize health and wealth as qualities of God, not of man. We joy in them as qualities of God. Whether we go into a prison, a hospital, a sickroom, or let the sick come to us, we behold only one Self, infinite in Its ministration.

From a great deal of experience working with men in prison, I have learned never to go into a prison seeing bad men, but also not to be so foolish as to look at those men and see good men. There is only one way: to see no man at all, but to see my Self. The Self that is the Self of me is the Self of them.

God, being infinite, God is the only Self. If God appears as Joel, God appears as James; if God appears as John, God appears as Mary: whoever it is, it is still God appearing.

I am not interested in any person's past. So far as I am concerned, the human history of any person is as uninteresting as most of the biographers of Jesus have found his early life to be. What interests us about Jesus is his Christhood, his Christ-mission, his Christ-message. What was he before he was thirty? A carpenter? A rabbi? What difference does it make? We know him as the Christ. We must arrive at that place in consciousness where we recognize that, regardless of what the appearance is, the Christ is the true identity of every individual—be he saint or sinner. If we see anyone as less than the Christ-selfhood, we are violating karmic law, and we must pay the penalty in our own demonstration of harmony because what we are beholding becomes the law unto us.

To Be Under Grace rather than Karmic Law, Live Spiritually

God is made evident, visible, and tangible as you and as me. There is no such thing as loving God unless we love each other. There is no loving God unless we forgive each other; there is no loving God while we hold each other in bondage to criticism, condemnation, or judgment. The higher we go in Christ-consciousness, the less we are tempted to judge, criticize, or condemn.

Karmic law never deviates; it never fails. We, ourselves, cannot deviate from it without suffering a reaction. True, this is the law of cause and effect and, therefore, it is purely in the human realm. That is correct: the law of cause and effect operates only on the human level of life; but let us not forget that while we are beholding good and evil we are on the human level of life. Once we have risen above the human sense of life into our Christhood, no one has to remind us of the Ten

Commandments or the Sermon on the Mount.

This does not give us the right to say, "Oh, I am living in my Christhood, so none of these human laws operate in my experience," and at the same time continue to live contrary to spiritual law. It is like the man I knew many years ago who enjoyed his cocktails every afternoon. When I seemed surprised at the pleasure he derived from them, he thought I was very narrow and bigoted, because what harm is there, what power could there be in a cocktail? I could only answer, "Well, that was what I was shocked about—the power of good you seem to be getting out of it. Do not try to tell me that there is no power for evil, but that there is power for good in the same thing. How can you say that alcohol has no power for evil, but that it has a power for good, and then in the next breath say that it has no power?" We do much the same thing in connection with the food we eat. We glibly mouth the words, "Oh, I am spiritual. I am not subject to any of these human laws." No? What about a quart of ice cream or two pounds of chocolates eaten at one sitting? "Oh," but you say, "that's different. That's good." No, as long as we are subject to laws of good, we are subject to laws of evil.

The New Creature

The qualities of good and of evil belong to the mortal sense of man which must "die daily"[4] in order that the other man may be reborn of the Spirit—the "new man,"[5] the "new creature"[6] in Christ. We are not a new creature in Christ if we are a good human being. We are a new creature in Christ if we are immortal spiritual being, and if we know this. A spiritual life does not indulge in human condemnation or human praise. Neither of these states of consciousness enters heaven.

"Why callest thou me good? There is none good but one, that is, God."[7] If I, by any chance, am an instrument through which God is doing good, then I am an instrument of God through which the good of God is flowing. Those individuals who at the moment may be instruments through which evil is being made manifest are but momentary instruments for that evil. Tomorrow they may be the saints of the world. Saul of Tarsus today becomes St. Paul tomorrow. The devil Augustine, that horrible, immoral character, becomes St. Augustine tomorrow.

Paul reveals that there is that within us which always wants to do evil when we want to do good. He acknowledges that even when he sins, it is not really he who is sinning, but this false sense that is in him. He, himself, does not wish to be a party to the sin, in fact, is rebelling at it, revolting against it. And so it is that we do not pray to God to lead us not into temptation; rather are we turning to that center within our own being and acknowledging to ourselves that we do not wish to sin, we do not wish to fear, we do not wish to doubt. Whatever the error is that is holding us in bondage, we are trying to break it and to be released from it.

The Spirit of God Breaking Through

Never believe that God is tempting us or holding us in bondage to sin because to do that it would be necessary for God to have a knowledge of sin. But if we turn within, asking for release, we do not know where that prayer or desire goes, but we know that we of ourselves never prayed to be released from temptation. We rather liked the temptation. No, it is the spirit of God breaking through to us and trying to get us to desire to be released from sin.

When we turn within and ask to be released from any error, it is God praying in us, trying to get us to release ourselves from these earthly desires, earthly fears, earthly troubles. No human being in and of himself wants to change from being a human being: human beings like their state of humanhood. Of course they would like it better if it were on an improved scale, nevertheless they like it. It is only when divinity touches us that a dissatisfaction creeps in to our humanness. Actually it is not we ourselves who are praying; it is not we ourselves who are turning to God. It is the spirit of God breaking through to us.

We are always trying to run away from God, but when we defy human circumstances that we may be given more spiritual light, in those moments God is gaining a victory over us. He is catching up with us. In our student days when we pray for light, we are not really praying to God: it is God trying to break through to us. When we pray, "Lead us not into temptation,"[8] it is not so much that we are praying as that God is praying, moving in us, to remove temptation or the desire for temptation from us. God never at any time has tempted anyone. I have spoken to many people who have attained a great measure of spiritual illumination, and not one of them has told me he was ever tempted to steal, commit adultery, hate his neighbor, fear for his life, or fear death—not one of them. They do not seem to have been troubled by what may have tempted us. In their spiritual illumination they have come into a realization of God and they have found a kingdom in which there is no temptation—physical, mental, moral, or any other kind—just no temptation.

Temptation

God does not tempt us, but in our struggles upward we are tempted, but that temptation is of the world, not of God. Lot's wife was tempted to turn around and go back to the very world she was leaving. Jonah was tempted. Many are tempted on their upward path to turn back and sometimes that temptation comes in the form of health or prosperity, but it is not God who is tempting them. It is worldliness tempting them to remain in the world.

It was not God who tempted Jesus on the heights. It was the world that tempted him in the form of personal sense appearing as the devil. It was the desire to display his ego in making demonstrations. That was the tempter. Personal sense is the tempter, not God. Personal sense tempts us to claim to be creators of good or evil. Personal sense tempts us to want physical ease. Personal sense tempts us in many directions but God never tempts us.

In spiritual awareness, there is no temptation: there is only the desire to let love flow, to live in love, to love and to be loved. No sense of wrongdoing is ever connected with the spiritual life. Every experience of the spiritually illumined is a spiritual impulse prompted by love. It may be misinterpreted or misunderstood by the world, but what it is, is love. It is never temptation; it is never done with any sense of temptation. Never is it God who tempts us. Always when there is temptation, it is personal sense. How can we know that we are living this spiritual life? When our promptings are not connected with a sense of guilt, that is when we know it is not personal sense that is prompting some act but it is God.

Rising into My Kingdom

As this spiritual sense is realized, we do not overcome jealousy, envy, or sensuality: we come into a kingdom where none of these things exists because there is no personal sense to be catered to, to receive anything, to need anything, to want anything. There is only the one Self. How can we give anything to a person who has attained "My kingdom," and how can a person who has attained that kingdom have anything left to get, desire, or want? How can a person who has attained spiritual consciousness have any awareness of incompleteness. In the attainment which takes place in that split-second of transition, God is revealed as fulfillment, and so there are no desires; there is no future: there is only this second, lived twenty-four hours a day in which nothing can be added to us, nothing can be taken from us. Ah, there it is. That is the point of spiritual unfoldment: nothing can be added to us. Because of that, there is no desire: we have fulfillment and in fulfillment, what is left for us to desire? What can we get? What can be withheld from us? Nothing!

Grace Appears as the Fulfillment of the Moment

That which exists at the center of our being is Spirit. It unfolds spiritually, but in unfolding spiritually, it provides for our daily needs. It makes no difference how material the object may seem to be that is necessary for our immediate fulfillment—dollars, bread and butter, meat, housing, transportation—it makes no difference what its nature, it is not necessary for us to take thought about its attainment. It will automatically appear as it is needed.

We do not ever think of ourselves as being honest—such a thought would not ever enter our mind—but if we went to a bank and changed a ten dollar bill and the teller gave us twelve one dollar bills for our ten, we would turn around and hand back two. We would not first say, "I am honest"; we would just automatically turn around with, "You have made a mistake." As the innate integrity that is always present is called upon for expression, it appears. The moment the spiritual integrity to which we never refer and of which we never speak or even think is called for in visible expression, it appears.

We need take no thought for the morrow, for what we shall eat or what we shall drink or wherewithal we shall be clothed. This Spirit that is within us will always appear at the second when It is needed in visible expression, and It will appear as the form necessary at that moment, whether it is in the form of honesty that gives back those extra two dollars, or whether it is in the form of a loaf of bread, the form of a dollar bill, the form of a berth on a steamer, or a seat on a plane. Whatever form is necessary, and regardless of how material it may seem to our sense, it will be there. It will be there in proportion as we relax from the word "I." I, the personal I, am not responsible for my daily bread—*I* am; God is, the Spirit is. As long as we maintain the personal sense of I, just so long do we not permit the Spirit to operate.

If we maintain our relationship with one another in accord with spiritual integrity, then we ourselves fulfill ourselves and we have nothing else to consider. In other words, I must maintain myself in such a way as not to fulfill what someone else would like to have me do, but so that I fulfill my highest sense of spiritual good. You, on the other hand, have no right to take into consideration what my conduct toward you is, you should take into consideration only what your own sense of integrity is so that you fulfill that sense of integrity, regardless of how much I may or may not deserve it. Any lack of integrity on my part brings about its own punishment within me just as any lack of integrity in you has a similar effect on you.

We stand or fall on our own spiritual integrity or lack of it. What is spiritual integrity? It is the realization that there is only one Self. Your Self is my Self. The evil we do to another, we are doing to ourselves. In the realization of the oneness of all life, there is no condemnation: "Neither do I condemn thee; go, and sin no more."

Chapter Three

Letting God Reveal Itself

The Master tells us, "My kingdom is not of this world,"[1] and that we are not to take thought for what we should eat, drink, or how we should be clothed. We take no thought for those things because those things are of "this world," but instead we take thought for My kingdom, the kingdom of God that is within. As we dwell—live and move and have our being—in that kingdom, all the affairs of this world are taken care of by a divine influence that is within us and are carried forward by a divine impulsion.

As long as we continue to take thought for the things of this world, we miss the way. That does not mean to become impractical and to stop being sensible businessmen or good housekeepers. It does not mean that at all. We continue to carry on all our normal human activity, but we do it without concern, without anxiety, doubt, or fear, since we are consciously aware that as long as we abide in the spiritual kingdom there is a spiritual presence functioning in us to perform that which is given us to do. This may sound more difficult than it is. What it really means is that we are not to neglect any of our duties or responsibilities, but to fulfill them in the assurance that there is a something greater than ourselves working within us to fulfill our lives.

Is There God?

There is an ancient wisdom originally given to disciples of many spiritual saints and seers, and this wisdom is: God is. To you or me, however, it is of no concern at this moment what God is, how God operates, or why. There is but one question that is important to us and it is a question upon which our whole existence depends: Is there God or is there not God? If there is no God, it becomes our duty to use every human means available to achieve happiness, harmony, and success in our daily lives. But if there is God, then the responsibility is upon Its shoulder; the government is in Its hands.

As the question of whether there is a God or not presents itself to us, the answer must come back from within our own heart: "Yes, God is." We may not know *what* God is. We may never have seen or felt God function. We may not have enjoyed the things of God, the care of God, the protection of God, the healing of God. So far in our life these things may all have evaded us. Nonetheless something within the depth of our being says, "And yet God is." God is, that we know. Why we have missed the way, why we seem to have been left out, we do not know. Perhaps we do not even know why we are convinced that God is. Perhaps we have no sensible reason for it. Perhaps if we were compelled to explain to an atheist why we are convinced that there is God, we would have no words with which to do it. Perhaps we would not be able to reason it out.

In spite of all that our hearts still say, "God is." For us, that can be sufficient. For us the whole weight of human life may fall away by just the simple acknowledgment that God is, because included in that statement would be the realization that, if God is, then all is well. If God is, then there is God-government, God-life, God-law, God-guidance, God-direction. As long as we have the assurance that God is, we can safely drop concern, fear, and doubt for this world.

Why Many Have Not Experienced God

One reason we have never experienced the fullness of God is that most of us have never taken the fifteen, twenty, or thirty minutes necessary to sit back with that simple question: Do I know that God is—not merely do I believe in God? Certainly, I believe in God. I am afraid not to believe in God for fear something terrible will happen to me, but my belief has never done me much good.

The question is not whether I believe in God or do not believe in Him. The question I am asking myself now is: Is there a God? I cannot answer that question with my mind. I cannot answer it with what my parents taught me or what my minister taught me. I must wait for my heart to answer it. I am no longer satisfied with what man tells me about God, religion, or spiritual things. I am now at the point where I wish to be taught of God. I wish to know now that what the Master taught about the kingdom of God being within me is true. I wish now to experience being taught by God, having God speak to me as directly as God spoke to Moses, Elijah, Elisha, Isaiah, Jesus, John, Paul.

To Whom Is God Available?

"God is no respecter of persons."[2] God does not pick out a few saints to talk to and neglect the world. God does not select a few practitioners or teachers for inner communion. God is available to every man, woman, child, animal, and plant in the entire realm. "God is no respecter of persons." God is omnipresent where I am and where you are. "The place whereon thou standest is holy ground."[3] God is as close to me as my breathing and as near as my hands and feet. Therefore, when we pray, we go into the inner sanctuary of our being and close the door, close our eyes and ears, close out this world, and there acknowledge:

I know there is a God.
I know there is a God at hand.
I know there is a God available to me
here where I am. The very place whereon I stand
is holy ground. It makes no difference
if at the moment I have climbed up to heaven
or have made my bed in hell, or if
"I walk through the valley of the shadow of death,"[4]
still I know the place whereon I stand is holy ground.
I know that where I am, God is;
I know that God longs to impart Himself to me.

So I need know nothing more about God than God is, and then have the quietness and patience to listen for that "still small voice,"[5] and be obedient to Its leading even though at the moment I may not know why.

Dare to Do and to Be

Never fear to make a mistake while following God because any mistake you make will be corrected without injury to anyone. Most of the failures in life have been because people were afraid to make mistakes. They felt that everything they had to do must be perfect, and that is not true. Place your whole heart, soul, and mind, your whole reliance on the Infinite Invisible, and then dare to do and to be, and fear no mistakes because God will correct them in time to save you and all others from any serious tragedy. Learn not to be afraid of mistakes and you will make less of them. Never fear to dare, because in the name and nature of God and with complete confidence in God's nearness, we can dare; we can be original.

What has brought us our problems on earth is a lack of understanding of God and God's nature. As long as we ascribe to God qualities of good and evil, we are not understanding the nature of God. As long as we think of God as that which can give or that which can withhold, we do not yet know the nature of God. God neither punishes nor rewards.

God is one. "Hear, O Israel: The Lord our God is one Lord,"[6] one power, one life, one love—without deviation, opposition, or contradiction. God is one. All that emanates from God is love, life, truth, safety, security, peace, joy, harmony, prosperity, success, spiritual completeness. Nothing but good emanates from God. We need not look to God for anything else. God is fulfillment within us. God fulfills Himself in our joy, our success, our peace, our harmony. Not knowing this truth we have separated ourselves from the fruitage of spiritual knowledge. If we know this truth it will make us free.

God's Love Wipes Out All Our Mistakes and Failures

God does not reward and God does not punish, nor does God visit good or evil upon anyone. God does not send life. God does not send death. God neither gives nor withholds. God is spiritual good forever expressing Itself as good. Never fear to come into God's presence because you have sinned or because you are sinning. Do not believe for a moment that God will withhold Itself because of your past or present sins.

Regardless of your present status, never hesitate day after day to retire into your sanctuary and abide there in God's presence. Let God envelop you, enfold you, permeate you. Let God's love reveal Itself to you. Let the voice of God utter Itself to you. Then you will be shown the way to make amends for your past sins and to experience absolution for your present ones. Though your sins are scarlet, you are white as snow the very moment you turn with deep conviction to the Father within and surrender yourself to the Father, even though you may sin again, tomorrow, next week, next year. That is part of the mesmerism of human life.

Should you fall by the wayside, physically, mentally, morally, financially, should you behold others on the spiritual path temporarily fall by the wayside, or should you even find your practitioner or teacher in some momentary sin, fear, lack, or disease, be sure that you do not judge, criticize, or condemn. Remember that this world is a state of mesmerism that often touches those even in high places as it did with Judas. Judas must have been a very reliable and spiritual character or the Master would never have chosen him for three years of discipleship. But in spite of every good opportunity, the mesmerism of the world was such that Judas fell, and he fell a little too hard.

Peter fell also. He fell to the extent of denying the Master three times, of hiding away when the Master was in his greatest trouble, and yet the Master knew that the temptation of the world is such that that could happen. As soon as Peter regretted and turned back again to the Master, the Master forgave him. Thomas also came under the world-mesmerism, and he too sinned, sinned against the Master, sinned against God, sinned against the Holy Ghost in that he doubted. He actually doubted the allness of God. He doubted immortality. He doubted the resurrection. He doubted the Master, Christ Jesus, and yet he must have been forgiven because he was permitted to continue as one of the disciples even after the Master had left the scene.

In God's Love There Is No Condemnation

So it is with you and me. In our spiritual identity we have a spiritual integrity which has never been violated. In our spiritual identity we are as pure as a newborn babe. Never have we sinned in our inner spiritual being. The sins of the flesh were sins of ignorance. The fears were fears of ignorance and usually stemmed from false teaching. Now when we come back to the Father's house to learn of the nature of God, this is what we learn: God neither punishes nor rewards. God is divine being, forever being Itself, forever bestowing Its grace, never giving it, never withholding it, but always expressing it. God's grace is omnipresent where we are at this moment and available to us the moment we turn within:

Father, I surrender all that I have believed.
I surrender every belief that does not testify to
Your presence, Your power, and Your love.
I no longer believe in reward and punishment.
I no longer believe that You send good and evil.
I no longer believe that God's will is that man should
experience accident, sin, or death—
not even for punishment of his crime.

Not even for his sins do I believe that God
sends sickness, death, accident,
disease, lack, or limitation.
I do not believe that God created these,
maintains or sustains them.
These all represent a state of belief in a selfhood
apart from God. In the eyes of God
there is no disease, no sin, no fear,
no punishment, no condemnation.
"There is therefore now no condemnation to them
which are in Christ Jesus,"[7]
who are in the realization of
their spiritual identity and their spiritual sonship.

I look out upon this world and I see men
suffering what appears to be punishment,
but now I know that it is
not a punishment of God's making.
Man is punishing himself
because of his own guilt complex.
God never punishes.
God never visits sickness, death, hell,

> poverty, or slavery upon anyone on the face
> of the globe. God maintains His creation intact
> within Himself, and it is our privilege to awaken.
> "Awake thou that sleepest, and arise from the dead,
> and Christ shall give thee light."[8]

Awake now, you who sleep. Awake now, you who have believed in orthodox teachings of rewards and punishments or a visitation of evil by God, or of vengeance by God. Throw all of that out; it never was true. Such language was used in the Old Testament just as parents sometimes use that language to their little children in training them when they say, "God will punish you," or "Mama will punish you." I do not know what you believe about God's punishment, but I know you could never believe that Mama will ever punish anybody, a little correction but never punishment. As a parent, you would never visit insanity, accidents, or a horrible disease upon your children. Your heavenly Father is the source not only of your love but of that greater love which is God's love for His creation. How then can you believe that God would punish man? Never again accept the doctrine of punishment.

Sin Brings Its Own Penalty

When you sin knowingly or unknowingly, it carries a penalty because it is in itself a violation of your own understanding. But that punishment lasts no longer than your own realization of the error of your ways, "Repent, and turn yourselves from all your transgressions. . . . For I have no pleasure in the death of him that dieth, saith the Lord God: Wherefore turn yourselves, and live ye."[9]

In any moment, turn and seek the realization of God's continuous love and realize that in Him there never has been criticism, judgment, or condemnation. The Master, Christ Jesus, knew this probably better than any man. When asked by his disciples, "Master, who did sin, this man, or his parents? . . . Jesus answered, Neither hath this man sinned, nor his parents."[10] "Neither do I condemn thee: go, and sin no more."[11] Jesus above all men knew that we must forgive seventy times seven, and he knew that God's forgiveness is seventy times seventy times seven. In other words, God's forgiveness is endless. Why? Because God does not hold us in condemnation, criticism, or judgment. "Who made me a judge or a divider over you?"[12]

All Erroneous Acts, a World-Mesmerism

So if there are past sins, drop the penalty for them in this moment and realize they are as dead as yesterday. They can never live again unless you revive them in your memory. Outside of your memory they have no existence. So the sins do not exist; the punishment does not exist. And what of those sins with which we are burdened today and which we may repeat tomorrow? Each time the world-mesmerism is so great that if it compels us, even against our better desires and judgment, to sin again, let us turn within in the realization, "Father, that is no part of my true being. That is no part of Your true being; therefore, it is not held against me, and with the grace of God it is dead in me now."

It may be necessary to repeat that every time the sin appears, and it may appear for a day, a week, a month, a year. Each time we must go back until the world-mesmerism has dropped away and we are as pure in action as we have desired to be. There is not an individual who is not 100 percent pure in heart and who does not desire to carry that purity into the world in thought and act. There is probably not one of us, however, who is completely pure in thought and deed. But the degree of our impurity is only the degree that world-mesmerism, world belief, has impinged itself upon us and compelled us to think and act in world terms. From the many students with whom I have worked, I know that regardless of their offenses, not one willingly wants to offend.

Begin Each Day Anew

Always it is the world-mesmerism that forces us to think and do what we do not wish to do. Paul recognized that: "For the good that I would I do not: but the evil which I would not, that I do."[13] And so it is with all of us. When we make that acknowledgment, we are recognizing that in our hearts, at least, our desires, aims, hopes, and ambitions represent absolute spiritual purity. So in that sense we can turn every day if necessary to the Father within and say, "Let me begin this day anew. Do not let me carry over from yesterday any memory of my offenses. Let me begin anew." You will find, as many have, that in the days, weeks, or months ahead that most of the world's evils will depart from you. The few that remain are the few that are so strong in race consciousness or universal consciousness that we have to be faithful to our inner selves to reach ultimately that day of complete purity, the day which none of us has yet achieved on earth.

Not looking back, Paul says, "Forgetting those things which are behind, and reaching forth unto those things which are before, I press toward the mark for the prize of the high calling of God in Christ Jesus."[14] Not claiming to have arrived at absolute Christhood but forgetting those things which are past, we turn now to the future. And if we stumble again, we will forget those things which are past and look again to the future. It rests with you as an individual, as it does with me, to find within our hearts that God is, that God is forever giving Itself to us, regardless of whether we are up or down, sick or well, rich or poor, saint or sinner. God is giving Itself to us.

In that realization, neither holding God nor ourselves in condemnation, the day eventually comes when we find ourselves very often consciously one with God in conscious awareness of God's bounty, grace, love, and peace. These we share with one another by entertaining no criticism, no judgment, of each other, and desiring no punishment for anyone. Regardless of the nature of their sins of this moment, always be willing to realize:

> "Father, forgive them; for they know not
> what they do."[15] Father, do not hold them
> in condemnation for their errors.
> Do not visit punishment upon them.
> Do not permit punishment to be visited upon them,
> but hold them in Thy grace
> and open their eyes to Thy love and Thy light.

We, who are reading this message, must forever abide together in that relationship, always remembering that we are of one mind in one place in consciousness, receiving a message of love and grace from God in our hearts. We must forever permit that love which is flowing to us from God to flow to one another. When we learn enough of love so that we can hold each other in this sacred relationship, then we will be able to go out and begin to take in our fellow man in our community life, family life, national life, and ultimately international life. The day must come when God's love will cover the earth through you and through me. In this consciousness of love there is neither Jew nor Gentile: there is only the child of God, the spiritual son, the divine revelation of God's government.

Once a year the Hebrews have a Day of Atonement. On that day they seek God's forgiveness and they believe that all their sins of the past year are forgiven and that they start out with a new slate absolutely clean. The Roman Catholics have more than one Day of Atonement because every time they go to their priest for confession they are forgiven their sins and they start out anew. We do not have any such consolation because we start out with the understanding that God does not punish us for our sins and, therefore, God has no forgiving to do. If we are to be forgiven our sins and have a clean slate, it rests with us in the integrity of our inner being to surrender ourselves in the realization that we actually, really and truly, have come to a point of decision in which we no longer want to sin, fear sin, or will commit sin. But it must be an inner conviction because we do not have to convince God. We have to convince ourselves that we are honest in seeking this clean slate.

Seek your own inner integrity and convince yourself that your desire is to be sinless and pure. Then you will have your own day of atonement, as many days in the year as may be necessary, and you will immediately begin to partake of God's grace, which is never withheld from you.

No Separation from God

Never forget the word *is*. Be aware of it on every occasion, every minute of every day. You are not to seek God. You are not to search for God. You are not to run after God. You are not to attempt to contact God. You are to remember that God already is and the contact is already intact. All that you are expecting of God, God already is. All that you are desiring of God, God already is.

Infinite Way writings may use such terminology as "You must contact God," or "You must make a contact with God," or "You must seek God," or "You must search for God." That is the language used for beginners, so that they may be led to the realization of the need for God in their immediate experience.

As students advance in understanding, however, they must eventually come to a place where they know that God already is "closer. . . than breathing and nearer than hands and feet,"[16] so they do not have to go after God, or search for God. You who are students must know sometimes that "the place whereon thou standest is holy ground," not tomorrow, not after you have read some books, not after you are given treatments, not after you go through classes. No, the purpose of class is to reveal to you that God is closer than breathing this minute, that "the place whereon thou standest" is already holy ground because

God is already there, that God is already the life of your being, the soul of your being, the substance of your being.

Everything in the spiritual universe revolves around the word *is,* as in the 23rd Psalm: "The Lord is my shepherd; I shall not want."[17] In that, there is no reaching out to God, no demanding anything. It is an assurance that the Lord is close at hand. The Lord knows my need before I ask; therefore, I shall not want. *Is* is the sacred word of all time.

God is within me.
God knows my needs before I do.
God is forever functioning as the harmony
of my being and as the eternality of my life,
as the infinity of my supply,
and as the divinity of my being.
God is already harmony, eternity, infinity.

Never set up a sense of separation between God and you, for you will set up a sense of separation between you and your demonstration. You cannot experience the peace, the joy, and the life of God while you are thinking that God is separate from you or God is punishing you, and you have to get back into God's grace. That is not true. You are at this moment enfolded in God, and God is enfolded in you. I in you, and you in me, and both of us in God. That is our relationship now, not after some event takes place, not after certain teachings or treatments. "Now are we the sons of God."[18] Now do we live and move and have our being in God's presence. Now are these things true.

God Is

The realization of God's omnipotence, omniscience, and omnipresence is what purifies us of our sins, diseases, lacks, and limitations. Seeking God will not do it. Seeking God is for the beginner who has not yet learned that God is "closer. . . than breathing, and nearer than hands and feet." Seeking and searching are for the beginner who does not know where he may find his God. But the student who no longer searches or seeks rests in the realization of God's presence, rests in the realization of God's love.

Whither shall I go from thy Spirit?
or whither shall I flee from thy presence?

If I ascend up into heaven, thou art there:
if I make my bed in hell, behold, thou art there.

If I take the wings of the morning,
and dwell in the uttermost parts of the sea;

Even there shall thy hand lead me,
and thy right hand shall hold me.

Psalm 139:7-10

Relax in the realization of God's law as being right here and now where you are. Do not hesitate to say this to the sinner in prison. Do not hesitate to say this silently to those bound in mental institutions. Do not hesitate to know this truth about those who are bedridden and diseased. Regardless of all appearances, God is, God is the life of every individual, and God is the soul. If you cannot remember any prayer or treatment when you are called upon for help for yourself or for others, if you just repeat that one word *is,* and are satisfied, you would find it a very complete treatment—just the word *is.* If you must go further, God *is,* and that is enough.

All the troubles in the world are based on the belief that we do not have a God at hand, that we have strayed from God, that God is not maintaining us or sustaining us in His own image and likeness, that we have sinned and we cannot be well until we get back into God's grace. We have never left God's grace. God does not know that we entertain a sense of separation. God does not know that we have ever physically, mentally, morally, or financially sinned. God does not know that we have been unjust. "Thou art of purer eyes than to behold evil, and canst not look on iniquity."[19]

Evil of all kinds transpires in what we call our Adam-dream, our human sense of existence, our sleeping state. When we awaken we find it never happened: God has always been where we are. There is no more powerful treatment or prayer or realization than that one word *is.* You can smile when you say, "Is," because it is a joyous occasion to realize that "though your sins be as scarlet, they shall be as white as snow,"[20] because God is where you are, and God is the purification of your being.

All of this we bring into our experience through the conscious recognition and realization of it within us. No man can do this for us; no teacher can do it for us. A teacher can present the principles of life to us. The teacher can lift us higher in consciousness than we were before so that we can spiritually discern these truths, but then each one goes off by himself and lives his own life. He then has the responsibility to live and move and have his being in this truth. That is why the Master said, "It is expedient for you that I go away: for if I go not away, the Comforter will not come unto you."[21] If you keep on depending on a teacher, or on Jesus, or on some master, you will not come into the realization of this *isness* of life, this realization of God's presence and His power. So each one of us must assume the responsibility for living in the word *is:* God is. That is all. God is; all is well. The day comes when that is such a complete realization that never again does a question about it come to your awareness.

Tape Recorded Excerpts
Prepared by the Editor

What is God to you? A vague something or other to which you give lip service because of years of theological indoctrination? Or has God become for you a living experience, permeating every fabric of your being? Ask yourself: What is God to me? Do I know God? What do I really know of that divine companion that is forever with me, always pouring forth Its irrepressible love and compassion? How often do I take time to listen to Its comforting, healing, renewing, and regenerating words?

When such questions form the core of one's meditation day after day, and when one is not satisfied with easy, pat answers welling up out of the mind, which are merely the residue of desultory reading, rich is the reward in greater awareness. The excerpt from the recordings below will be of help to you:

"What Is God to You?"

"There is a difficulty that everyone has to surmount if he is to remain on the spiritual path. That difficulty concerns itself with two words. Once you have been able to rise above the limitations of these two words, you will find that the spiritual path is much easier than you had ever believed, much more joyous and very fruitful. But the struggle for awhile is with these two words.

"The first of these words is 'God'. This is the most difficult part of your spiritual journey because it is difficult to rise above the concepts of God that you have accepted. Whether you received your concept of God from a church, from a parent, or from your own experiences in life—regardless of where you received your concept of God, regardless of how you received it, and regardless of what that concept of God may be—it is not God, and therein lies the first difficulty.

"There is nothing that you know about God that is God.

There is no idea of God that you entertain that is God. There is no possible thought about God that you have that is God. It makes no difference what your idea may be or what your concept may be, it remains an idea or a concept that is not God. And so, the young student must eventually realize that he has to rise above every concept of God before he can have an experience of God . . . .

"Every concept of God has failed to bring peace on earth, not only collectively but individually, and it is for this reason that we have a world of unrest. . . . Regardless of what concept of God you may entertain and regardless of how correct it may be, it still will not give you freedom, peace, safety, or security. Only one thing will bring to an individual, and ultimately to the world, absolute safety, security, freedom, justice, and equality, and that one thing is the God-experience—not a theory about God, not a concept of God, not an idea of God, but a God-experience."

Joel S. Goldsmith. "God, Prayer, Grace,"
The 1960 New York Open Class. Tape 1:2.

Chapter Four

Progressive Unfoldment

When you first embark on a spiritual or religious way of life, questions regarding the meaning and use of certain words will inevitably arise. You cannot speak without using words and as you know from consulting any unabridged dictionary, the same word may have many meanings and sometimes not even similar meanings, depending on how it is used. When it comes to religious terminology, this is even more true because people of many different religions use the same words, such as a word like "God", and they believe in that God. But if you were to ask a Roman Catholic about God, you would have one answer, from a Protestant another answer, from a Hebrew still another, from a Vedantist a quite different one, and those following the teachings of Shankara or Zen Buddhism would give even other meanings for God. Yet they all use the word God, and it means something different to each one.

In metaphysics the word "Christ" has a different meaning from its meaning in orthodoxy, and the word "prayer" is hardly recognizable from its dictionary meaning. Prayer to most people is a petition to God for something. To other people it is an affirmation of truth. To still others it is wordless but with inner thought, and then to others it is wordless and without thought.

So prayer has different meanings for different persons. This is true of every question that has been raised in regard to the Bible.

As you study the various approaches to truth, you will find that the teachers use the same words, but that each approach gives to those words its own special meaning. So it is in the Infinite Way. We do not always agree with others on the meaning of words, and others do not agree with us. That is understandable. The main thing is that we ourselves understand what we mean when we use certain words, statements, thoughts, or truths.

Affirmations of Truth or Reminders?

Affirmations are sometimes used in truth-teachings, that is, a repetition of the same statement over and over again with the idea of impressing it on consciousness. In the Infinite Way, we do not do that. We will take a statement which might be looked upon as an affirmation but, rather than use it as an affirmation, we use it as an application of a truth to a specific situation. For example, if I am faced with many problems out here in the world and I become very still, a Bible quotation, such as, "Greater is he that is in you, than he that is in the world,"[1] may come to my thought. We would not use that quotation as an affirmation to repeat, but as a reminder: "Ah yes, there is a He within me that is greater than all the problems with which I am faced today." Realizing that, we can forget the problems and the quotation, and just remember that there is a He within me and rest in that.

If I am faced with a great deal to meet during the day, it may come to me, "He performeth the thing that is appointed for me."[2] I would never think of using that as an affirmation and repeating that statement over and over, but, if it came to my thought, I would then turn to it in the sense of reminding myself that I am not called upon to do this work today. He that gave it to me to do also performs it, and then the problem drops from thought.

The statement, "Thou wilt keep him in perfect peace, whose mind is stayed on thee,"[3] should never be used as an affirmation, but rather to call our attention to the need for obedience to it. So, knowing that, I do not need the statement anymore. What I need now is to keep my thought stayed on God, to act out that quotation by actually keeping thought stayed on God and not on the statement. Such admonitions as "Lean not unto thine own understanding. In all thy ways acknowledge him, and he shall direct thy paths"[4] would be of little value as an affirmation to be repeated. Instead remember:

God is the source of my supply.
God is the source of my breakfast, lunch, and dinner.
God is the power going with me
on my way today. God goes before me to
"make the crooked places straight."[5]
God is the wisdom of my being;
God is the soul of my being;
God is the eternality of my being.

In that remembrance I am acknowledging Him in all my ways. I do not have to repeat the statement. So it is that we do not use statements of truth in a repetitive sense. That does not mean that such a practice has no value. It may have for those who use it, but in the Infinite Way we use a statement of truth merely as a reminder of the essence of it and then attempt to ponder it rather than to continue repeating it. This does not imply a criticism of other methods or interpretations because there are different meanings sometimes for the very same thing.

Let the Manna of Spiritual Unfoldment Be a Daily Experience

In our work there is no labeling of any religious practice as right or wrong. What might be right for one individual would not be for another. What might be right for us at one stage of our unfoldment might not be right for us a year later. We have to progress in our unfoldment even within the area of our own particular teaching. In other words, we must not accept any part of our understanding as final. We accept our understanding of it today, but we may put an entirely different interpretation upon it next year.

When a discussion arises, as it sometimes will, as to the meaning of certain points, the best thing to do is not to depend on our knowledge, that of the dictionary, or on our knowledge of the terminology used in metaphysics. The best thing to do is to turn to the Father within and ask for an interpretation of it. Then we will get the answer suitable to our own unfoldment at any particular moment or stage.

There are some ideas in all metaphysical teachings that are of no value to the beginner. They are true and they are profound, but the beginner will not know how to interpret them any more than a high school boy would know how to apply himself to a college course. There is "milk"[6] for the babes and "meat"[7] for the adult even in a spiritual sense. What may sound right to a beginner and be right for him would never do for one at a later stage.

If we are satisfied with yesterday's manna, with yesterday's understanding, with yesterday's interpretation, we will not progress, and we must progress. It seems that I never go along more than six months without coming to the realization that I have to start all over again, that what I knew of truth before is no longer true or helpful, and now I have to begin all over and learn from the beginning. That is exactly what happens. I have very blank periods, usually not more than six months apart, in which I get to a point of frustration, during which I know that I am going nowhere and I am getting there very rapidly. The best thing to do in such a predicament is to turn to the Father and ask for fresh manna.

Importance of Unknowingness

Through maintaining an attitude of unknowingness, bit by bit scripture has revealed itself to me from a spiritual standpoint. It did not happen all at once. At one time when a student asked me about the 91st Psalm, I had to admit, "I don't know anything about it. I have read it and read it and I can't understand it or figure it out. It doesn't seem true to me, so I am not going to talk about it until an understanding comes." Shortly after that I opened the Bible to the 91st Psalm and it was as if I were reading it for the first time, especially the first sentence: "He that dwelleth in the secret place of the most High shall abide under the shadow of the Almighty."[8] As that first verse came alive, it changed the entire Psalm and made it all clear to me. Up to that time what had puzzled me was that the 91st Psalm told about how the evils of the world would not "come nigh thy dwelling."[9] But they did. Most of them had come nigh mine and that of many other persons that I knew. Yet here was the 91st Psalm saying that this would not happen, and that is why I did not understand it.

But when I read that first verse I had the whole secret. It will come nigh you and it will come nigh me if we are not dwelling, living, moving, and having our being in God-consciousness. If we are not abiding in the Word and letting the Word abide in us, all the evils of this world can come near our dwelling place. It is only "he that dwelleth in the secret place of the most High" who is promised immunity from the discords of the world. Would it not have been foolish for me to try to explain the 91st Psalm when I had not realized its meaning myself? So it has been with all of the Bible. Passage by passage, incident by incident, it has revealed itself to me.

There is still a great deal that has not become clear, but I know from past experience that every once in awhile another statement will reveal itself to me in its spiritual import. The spiritual import of a statement is what interests me. I do not think it is very important to know whether Moses crossed the Red Sea, the Delaware, or the Amazon. I do not think it is too important to know when Moses led the Hebrews out of Egypt, but I do think it is important to know how it came about that Moses was able to demonstrate manna from the sky, water from the rocks, a cloud by day and a pillar of fire by night. I think that's very important, and that part of scripture revealed to me that it was the consciousness of truth understood by Moses. Moses knew "I Am That I Am."[10] His consciousness of truth appeared as every necessary bit of fulfillment. The moment I saw that, I went through the Bible and saw how the same thing applied to Elijah, Elisha, Jesus, Paul, Peter. All of these spiritual lights brought forth miracles, but all of them brought them forth in the same way: by their consciousness of truth. Their own consciousness of truth within appeared outwardly as manifestation, expression, or demonstration.

That is true of us today. Healing actually is not a change of a physical condition of the body, since we are not physicians. Healing is a change of consciousness, a transforming of the mind, a renewing of the mind so that the moment a higher degree of consciousness is attained, a higher sense of health and harmony is demonstrated in our outer experience. But the degree of demonstration is dependent upon our degree of spiritual enlightenment or spiritual consciousness.

Importance of Greater Awareness

In our work no student can ever get out of his study any more than he puts into it. If, as a student, you have come to a place of putting in one hour a day of study, you will draw out something like the equivalent of one hour a day of spiritual harmony. If you have come to a place of studying two hours a day, you can look forward to about four hours of good in your experience. When you arrive at the place where truth is maintained in your consciousness from arising in the morning to retiring at night and sometimes waking up in the middle of the night, then you can look forward to the continuity of the Christ-experience.

There is no one on the spiritual path who can get out of this more than he puts into it because there is no sympathetic God sitting around taking pity on one and giving anyone more than his consciousness entitles him to. Only in the degree of his consciousness can harmony be demonstrated. If students of law go to their classes at a university prepared by previous study, regardless of what the professor of law says, that student will grasp it, and the other students will be left wondering what it's all about. It is that way in spiritual work, too. The student who puts in the study, whether reading the word, hearing the word, praying over the word, pondering and meditating, or putting it into practice, will get ten times more in understanding than the ones who are skimping in their reading, studying, meditating, pondering, and practicing.

If you do not get the answers to some of the questions that arise, do not feel, however, that it will in any way hinder your demonstration, because actually it makes no difference whether you know these things or not. Most of the questions are not important. Most of the questions are not even important if you have the answers to them, and at best most of the questions are answered by someone's opinion or concept or belief; whereas, with patience and turning within, you can get the true answers directly from the Father within.

The Crucifixion as an Historical Event

Questions are bound to arise about the meaning of certain incidents in the Bible, however, especially in the life of the Master and in connection with the crucifixion. Historically, we know most of the facts regarding the crucifixion. Jesus was a member of the Essenes, a spiritual order antagonistic to some of the practices of the Hebrew church and its forms of worship.

Actually, the Essenes were fighting the Hebrew church. There is evidence of that in the Master's driving the moneychangers out of the temple.

The Hebrew church had the right to make complaints to the Roman authorities under whom it lived, and the Roman authorities agreed to punish those who were charged by the Hebrew authorities with offenses, especially if the charge involved any danger to the Roman Empire. The charge against Jesus was that he was threatening the Roman Empire by promising to set up a new kingdom. We know that the new kingdom he was preaching about was the kingdom of God within us. He was preaching that spiritual kingdom which is not of this world. But whether or not the Hebrew church authorities knew that, or whether they merely used Jesus' preaching of a new kingdom as the basis of their charge, they made the charge. The Roman authorities then sentenced Jesus to be crucified. So much for the historical story of the crucifixion.

Did Jesus with his uplifted consciousness feel pain at the crucifixion? If I were to say that I would not be surprised if Jesus did have pain, that would not necessarily be the truth. It would represent my idea of the situation, and I might be just as wrong as those who felt Jesus had risen above any physical sense of pain. It would not surprise me if he had felt at least temporary pain. Why? Do you remember how he went to his disciples and begged the Father to remove this cup from him, this trial, this ordeal, but finally surrendered all sense of self-preservation when he said, "Nevertheless not as I will, but as thou wilt."[11] He indicated his willingness to go through with it, but if possible he asked that this ordeal be removed, perhaps feeling it might even be too much for him. He knew that the experience called death, especially violent death, was not something to take lightly. It was a serious matter, an experience he had never had before. How could he know in advance how he would accept it? He knew enough to know that he did not want to go through it if there were any way to avoid it.

When he was taken by the soldiers and made to carry that heavy crucifix, we are not given any idea of a man carrying it as if he were just twittling it with his thumbs. Scripture indicates that it was a burden to him, a heavy weight on his shoulders, and if it were a burden, would it be surprising if he had had pain with the driving in of those nails or that sword thrust? We know that blood ran, so why should there not have been pain?

Jesus may have risen to that state of consciousness where he had no sense of pain, but I doubt that you or I will ever know that as a fact, and I doubt that it is important that we know it, because there can be no importance as to whether or not he felt pain. If he felt all the pain in the world it would not take one single thing away from the glory of his demonstration. The fact of the matter is that he was crucified. The fact of the matter is that to human sense he died, was lifted off the cross, was entombed, and then walked the earth again. What difference does it make whether he did it without suffering or whether he did it with great pain and great suffering? The evidence is that he did it with great pain because even when he came out he bore the marks of the nails and the wound in his side.

Crucifixion as an Experience of Consciousness

Spiritually, crucifixion is an experience that comes to every individual on the spiritual path if he or she pursues the spiritual path for any great length of time. There are two ways of embarking on the spiritual path. One is to get wet only up to the knees, to take it very gently and mildly and be satisfied with a little better health, a little better supply, and a little better happiness, and rest content there because if you go much further than that a price is going to be demanded of you, and a very severe price.

The Master often refers to that price in his teaching of "Straight is the gate, and narrow is the way, which leadeth unto life, and few there be that find it,"[12] because you have to leave your mother, brother, sister, and father. You have to leave all for *My* sake. You have to leave your "nets". Jesus commanded Andrew and Peter, "Follow me, and I will make you fishers of men. And they straightway left their nets."[13] I wonder if you know the meaning of that passage. What would you think is the most important thing in the life of a fisherman? His nets. Now, what is a fisherman without nets? Lost. He might as well be a carpenter without tools. And yet the Master commanded them to leave that which to them represented their very livelihood and the support of their family. That is a very stiff price to pay for being a disciple: to have to leave your family, your living, your mode of living, and trust to the Invisible.

The Master further describes the lot of the disciple when he tells you not to be concerned when you are persecuted: "Blessed are ye, when men shall revile you, and persecute you . . . for so persecuted they the prophets which were before you."[14] If you take on this robe, this mission, you may very well be persecuted. Jesus was called "a man gluttonous, a wine bibber, a friend of publicans and sinners."[15] Do you think people are going to do any less to you if you go far on the spiritual path? Do you think you are not going to be misunderstood? Do you think your motives are not going to be misunderstood and questioned? Do you think your conduct at times is not going to be misinterpreted? Indeed it is.

There is nothing this human world likes more than to spatter a little mud on the person who is setting himself up with a white robe, not that you or I will ever claim to have arrived at complete Christhood, but we are struggling toward it. Nevertheless, the very least mistake we make, people are going to say, "Oh, there is a truth-student. Look at what he is doing. Why, he is worse than we are." Every little mistake you make is going to be criticized and jumped on, and if you should be unfortunate enough to have a claim, that is going to be a bad thing because according to the world a truth-student should not have a cold, should not get sick, should not wear glasses. That is all nonsense. None of us has claimed anywhere to have achieved full Christhood. "Forgetting those things which are behind, and reaching forth unto those things which are before, I press toward the mark."[16] With Paul, we are struggling forward for greater and greater light until we do reach that day of perfected Christhood.

We as students are under no delusions about one another. We do not look upon one another or upon our teachers as if they had arrived at full Christhood. So, if a mistake is made, if an illness comes, if some temptation of the human world impinges, there is only one thing to do. Instead of criticizing the teacher, jump in and know the truth that helps to set him free.

It must inevitably be true that problems raise us higher than human peace. The Master said, "Think not that I am come to send peace on earth: I came not to send peace, but a sword."[17] At what do you think the Christ-sword is aimed? The very minute we want more than just a little better demonstration of life, the minute we want to transcend human demonstration to know God aright, that moment the sword of the Spirit begins to hack away at all our humanness, and not only at some of our human evils, but some of our human good too, some of those humanly good qualities that stand in the way of spirituality.

Crucifixion today may not take the form of being nailed to a cross physically, but you might be surprised to discover how many times your own students or others in the work nail you to a cross. It is inevitable because no one can fathom the mind of an individual who has left human modes and means to live and move and have his being on the spiritual path. That, to me, is the meaning of crucifixion.

Unfolding Understanding of Prayer

Prayer is not a subject that can be taught in six lessons. As you go more deeply into the study of the writings, you will better understand prayer from the standpoint of the Infinite Way. Then at some class you may be lifted into that spiritual awareness where you will spiritually discern its meaning.

Prayer is not a static word with only one meaning. Prayer, as far as we are concerned, has many meanings. When I take a passage of scripture into my thought, ponder it, think about it, seek its inner meaning, or seek to apply it to some specific experience, that can be considered as one form of prayer. Any knowing of the truth is a form of prayer. "Ye shall know the truth, and the truth shall make you free."[18]

In our spiritual healing work, treatment or contemplative meditation, which is a form of prayer, begins with the word God. Our treatments or meditations relate solely to God. If you ask me for help for a physical discord, you may or you may not mention the nature of the discord. To me, that is immaterial because I am not listening. But if it makes you feel better to get it off your mind and say it is rheumatism, a headache, or a foot ache, that is all right with me. Frankly, I would not remember two minutes later what you said because I was not listening when you said it. It's enough for me to know that you have asked for help. The moment you ask me for help I turn to the word God. God is my first word in treatment or prayer. The following meditation is not a formula, and I do not go through this particular treatment or meditation each time. I am merely illustrating.

God, God is the life of individual being;
therefore, life is eternal.
God is the substance of all form;
therefore, the body of God,
the body of individual being is spiritual and perfect.

God is the activity of the body; therefore,
there is no part of the body that can be underactive,
overactive, or inactive.

Since God is the activity of body, body cannot refuse
to act in accord with God's plan for body.

God is the only law.
If God is the only law, then all law is spiritual.
There is no law of disease,
no law of sickness, no law of matter.
If God is the only law or law-giver and
God is Spirit, all law is spiritual.
Therefore, there are no laws to maintain disease,
no laws to create it, or sustain it.
Disease, being without law, must collapse.
God is the only law.

By this time, I may feel that the meditation or treatment is complete, so I sit back in silence with that listening ear, and I remain in that listening attitude until I get a response. It may be a deep breath. It may be what I have called a "click." It may be a passage of scripture. It may be some statement of truth. It may be nothing but a weight falling off my shoulder or a sense of release. It may be that a smile comes to my face, a sigh that all is well. Whatever it is, I know that God is on the field, and the treatment is complete. This may be called a treatment, but we can also call it prayer or knowing the truth.

Our prayer or treatment consists of two parts: the truth that we know about God and then waiting for God to put the seal on it. We never know a truth about man, woman, child, or animal. Our knowing the truth is about God—the activity of God, the law of God, the substance of God, the life of God, the qualities of God, the activities of God—and we stay right there in that.

Asking for Spiritual Help

How does the treatment reach you or the person who has asked for help? To begin with, you are the one who brought yourself to that consciousness, and God is the all-knowing, infinite intelligence. It must certainly know that you are the one who came and you are the one to whom the realization must be brought. But it is your asking for help, your being brought into the consciousness of truth that brings the results to you. That is why in our work we very seldom allow one person to ask for help for another unless that person is so incapacitated that he cannot. If there is someone in your family so ill as to be unable to ask for help or so incapacitated that the person cannot make the contact, then you can do it but that is as far as you can go.

Some persons send us a list of names to pray for, but we cannot accept such requests. If a person himself makes the contact, he receives the answer. He has tuned in; therefore, he gets the blessing, like the woman who pressed through the throng and touched the robe of the Master. And he said, "Thy faith hath made thee whole."[19] What would have happened if somebody else had pressed through the throng and asked Jesus to pray for her is a question. On the other hand there was the incident in which the centurion asked for help for his servant,[20] and because of the contact between the centurion's servant and the centurion, the healing took place. That can happen too.

If you ask for help for your child, your mother, or someone very close to you who is incapacitated, you act as the link in the chain and the person needing the help received the benefit from it. The greatest assurance of a person's receiving help is when the person himself makes the effort to achieve the realization, makes the effort to reach the practitioner and to hold himself in spiritual union with the practitioner. Such a one receives the greatest benefit.

I have never at any time had a list and I do not at any time expect to have one. My way of working is entirely different from that of working with lists. There again, do not misunderstand that. Working with lists may be very productive of good. I wouldn't know because I have never tried them, but my way of work is working with one individual at a time.

When I am conducting a class, I am not working specifically for anyone. But, having prepared myself in meditation, having felt the inflow of the Spirit, knowing that much of the time the Spirit is flowing through me, it is inevitable that anyone who is tuned to it, receptive and responsive, must receive some degree of benefit from it. That may appear as spiritual enlightenment; it may appear as physical, mental, moral, or financial healing; it may appear as uplifted consciousness. But everyone with some measure of receptivity must benefit from the degree of consciousness which is flowing.

Conducting a Healing Ministry

The moment a person asks for help, he alone is in my consciousness, and every bit of truth that I know is specifically and individually for him. No one else is in my consciousness; no one else enters my consciousness. He has turned to my consciousness, and my consciousness responds individually to him. In the course of the day, the telephone rings many times and different persons ask for help. When they do, they individually and specifically receive my help—nobody else, only the one on the telephone.

When I turn from the telephone to open my mail and when I am reading a letter from a person, that person is the one who receives the benefit of the prayer or realization because only he is in my consciousness. The letter of that person is put in a pile, and sometime during the day or night I go to my dictaphone, take the letter to answer, and again that person is the only one in my consciousness. Therefore, he is the one receiving the benefit of the treatment, prayer, or communion, the benefit of my consciousness of truth. When the secretary picks up the mail, types it, and brings it back for my signature, I read it to see that it is correct and then sign it. That person is in my consciousness and is again receiving the uplifted consciousness, the truth of being, the prayer, or treatment. That is the way I work.

Students who go into the practice are always instructed to treat every person as an individual, meditating for him specifically when the person touches their consciousness and as often as he returns to their consciousness.

Through the daily and hourly practice of keeping the mind stayed on God and meeting every claim individually as it hits up against consciousness, the student's progressive unfoldment is assured.

Chapter Five

A Purified Consciousness

As we become receptive and responsive to the experience of God, we can embrace the whole universe within ourselves in meditation:

> This universe of God's creating is within me
> and within all being.
> God's love enfolds and upholds it.
> God's love enfolds all who are therein.
> God's love permeates this universe.
> All that exists in this universe God created,
> and it is spiritual.
> All that exists is of God,
> and God is the good unto this universe.
> Whoever it is, wherever it is,
> whatever it is, it is neither good nor evil but wholly
> spiritual, as of God.
> The good which is God permeates
> and maintains it. Every individual embraced
> in my consciousness is the son of God,
> the child of God, the offspring of God,

God's own creation—not good and not evil.
All those embraced in the spiritual universe are
of God and therefore spiritual.

Neither Good nor Evil in Form or Effect

We do not label anyone good or evil. We place no labels on anyone, nor will we label any condition as good or evil. The moment some form of physical, mental, moral, or financial discord comes into our thought, we strip away the label of good or evil. We see it as a condition that exists, but a condition that exists not as good and not as evil. With such an attitude, we let it be translated into that which it is and thereby behold a harmony or a wholeness where heretofore there was discord or disease.

Let us begin with this moment and remember that there is neither good nor evil in this world. Let us place no labels of good or evil upon anyone or anything. We acknowledge God as the only good, and we acknowledge that all that exists partakes of God's goodness. Regardless of any appearance that may be in our thought at this moment, we acknowledge that evil has no real or permanent existence. Whatever the appearance, we will call it neither good nor evil.

It is a state of duality to behold good and evil. Whatever we see as a person, situation, or condition becomes good or evil in proportion to our thinking it so. Something that is very good to one becomes very evil to another. There is neither good nor evil in anything in and of itself, but our thinking can make it so unto us. It is not a reality but an illusory experience which will seem real, painful, harmful, or destructive to those who entertain thoughts of evil and destruction.

To attain this state of consciousness, however, calls for a rebirth because it means that we must consciously make the agreement now that in this whole world of men, women, and children, in this world of many and varied conditions, there is neither good nor evil. God alone is good and God's goodness permeates all that exists. There is no evil in any condition; there is no evil in any circumstance; there is no evil in any person, because God, the infinite good, did not create evil, and there is no other creator.

Being Purified of the Belief in Good and Evil

If we have entertained an evil sense of some person or condition, let us in this moment of dedication purify ourselves of such beliefs. In all this world, there is not what appears as an evil person or evil condition that has within himself, herself, or itself any powers of evil regardless of what we may look upon. Regardless of what its appearance at this moment is to us, we will remove its sting and its seemingly destructive nature when we look upon the person or condition and know within ourselves, "You have no powers of evil, for there are none. Just as the world has mislabeled this it, or you, and says that it or you are evil, dangerous, and destructive, so I, also, have heretofore mislabeled you. Now I know such a label is not true. I know that in all this universe there is no person, thing, or condition that has any quality of evil in it, any power of evil, or any power of destruction. It is neither good nor evil, for only God is good."

"Though I walk through the
valley of the shadow of death, I will fear no evil,"[1]
for there is no evil in that condition.
There is no evil presence and there is no evil power.
Though I seem to be consumed with disease,
I will no longer fear it,
for it has within itself no element of destruction,
no element of pain, no element of death.
In and of itself it is nothingness.

All power is in God. I will not say of this condition
that it is good, nor will I say of it that it is evil:
I will say merely,
"It is nothingness; God is allness."
Everything else is nothingness.
God's allness and God's goodness and
God's power and God's law permeate me,
permeate this universe, and permeate all conditions.

Heretofore we have lived in a world of two powers. We have tried to acquire a good power and we have tried to get rid of an evil power. Now we will do neither. We will rest content in that which is. We will rest in the realization that, apart from God, there is no power; apart from God there is no good.

God's omnipotence, omniscience, and omnipresence
assure me that God's good permeates
all being, all cause, and all effect.
I will not judge by appearances, and
I will withhold all judgment as to good or evil
and merely acknowledge that God alone is good.
Even this that I have been fearing is not evil.
Even this that I have been hating is not evil.
Even this that I have wondered why it came to my
dwelling place, now I know is not evil.
It has no qualities of evil;
he or she has no qualities of evil. God alone is good.

This will lead us out of the world of duality, out of the old mistake of having a power of God and a power of a devil, a power of good and a power of evil, or a power of immortal and a power of mortal. This will lead us into the fourth dimensional Consciousness in which nothing is either good or evil for all that is receives its grace, glory, power, substance, cause, and law from God. All that is, is of God and therefore spiritual, above qualities and above quantities. In the realm of God there is neither quality nor quantity: there is only infinity, eternality, immortality, a divine state of being which has no opposites, is neither good nor evil, but is spiritual.

Recognizing the Glory of God Omnipresent

The miracles of grace come into our experience in proportion as we withdraw judgment and labels from the world of men and women, conditions, things, and circumstances and no longer speak the language of good or evil, no longer speak the language of comparison, but recognize God as the creative principle of all, and all as spiritual. "Not that which goeth into the mouth defileth a man,"[2] but that which emanates from our own consciousness. We will never again be able to blame a person, a circumstance, or a condition for the inharmonies of our life because we will recognize that nothing that goes into our experience defiles or makes a lie, nothing that "man, whose breath is in his nostrils"[3] can do to us makes a lie, but rather what emanates from our consciousness.

If we persist in living in the world of duality and calling some things good and some things bad, then that bread which we have cast upon the waters returns to us. Instead we retire to our own consciousness, look out at this world and say, "I withdraw all labels from you. I no longer see you as good or evil. I see you as of God, and I see God's goodness permeating you. I see God's goodness upholding and sustaining you. I see the law of God keeping you in perfect peace. I do not put labels of good or evil on you. No good or evil emanates from my consciousness, only the vision of God's spiritual perfection, maintaining a spiritual universe in eternal glory, having no glory of its own but showing forth God's glory, God's handiwork. 'The heavens declare the glory of God; and the firmament sheweth his handywork.'[4]"

We have no glory of our own: it is all God's glory. We should not call it good; we should not call it evil; we must call it spiritual, of God. God's grace does not remove disease: God's grace reveals to us that there never has been disease, that we have accepted the world's concept of good and evil and, therefore, we have demonstrated that. In our spiritual enlightenment, we will no longer label anything disease; we will no longer label anything evil; we will no longer believe that any condition has in and of itself a power of evil, destruction, or of pain since all power emanates from God.

We will no longer believe that there is a law of disease, since all law is spiritual. There is no good law and there is no evil law; there is only one law, spiritual law, the law of God which governs God's creation, and there is no other creation.

All that is made God made, and God saw all that He made and it was very good. Therefore, we must not be deceived by appearances and be tempted into believing that we must get rid of, or rise above, evil, error, or discordant conditions. No, we must come into the glory of God and realize that God made all that was made, and all that was made is maintained and sustained by Its creative principle which is God.

Regardless of appearances I will label nothing good;
I will label nothing evil:
I will label all things spiritual, of God.

Spiritual Purity

Spiritual vision will result in translating false appearances into an understanding of the divine harmony which is ever present. "Therefore if thou bring thy gift to the altar, and there rememberest that thy brother hath ought against thee; first be reconciled to thy brother, and then come and offer thy gift."[5] If at any time we attempt to pray or commune with God and remember that we are holding anything or anyone in our consciousness as being good or evil, we must stop right there and make peace within ourself by agreeing that nothing is good or evil. Only God is good. The infinity of God's goodness permeating all being leaves nothing of an evil or destructive nature. Then when we have made peace so that we are not warring within ourselves against a person, a thing, or a condition, we may return to our meditation and our communion:

Father, I come to You with clean hands.
I have naught against anyone
and I do not accept anyone or anything as evil.
Therefore no one has anything against me.
Now I am in Thy presence in my spiritual purity.
I am entertaining no evil concepts of person, thing,
or condition. I am at peace with all creation.

In that state of spiritual purity, the grace of God is enabled to permeate our mind, soul, being, body, and pocketbook. The grace of God is able to flow in a consciousness that is not divided against itself and is not at war with anyone or anything. God's grace is able to flow through a consciousness that is single pointed, that has only one presence and one power—no opposites and no opposition. In that state of consciousness prayer is answered.

While we have ought against someone or something as having evil qualities or propensities, while we believe there is a world of duality, someone or something is evil, has evil, can cause or produce evil, we are a house divided against itself. We are a state of consciousness at war within ourselves, and the grace of God cannot reveal itself in such a divided household. Now we must be of a single mind. We must see with a single eye. To do that we must withdraw the labels of good and evil from everything there is and acknowledge all good to be God, God alone to be good. If we vest anything with the power of evil, that is the only evil it has to react upon us. When we withdraw the label of evil from a person or a condition, since the person or condition has no power of evil within itself, there is no longer any appearance of evil or belief of evil to react upon us. A belief of evil entertained in our consciousness reacts upon us.

Sowing and Reaping

If we entertain a sense of evil toward a person, place, thing, circumstance, or condition, that sense of evil which we entertain is the sense of evil which returns to harm our being, our body, or our business. When we relinquish all sense of evil, when we refuse to vest anything with powers of evil, then our consciousness is purged of all sense of evil and there is no longer a sense of evil to operate in us, upon us, through us, or against us. "As he thinketh in his heart, so is he"[6] means that as a person is convinced in his consciousness, that is, whatever he entertains in his consciousness is what he draws unto himself. If he does not entertain any consciousness or sense of evil, then none can react upon him.

"Cast thy bread upon the waters: for thou shalt find it after many days."[7] Cast your understanding of oneness upon the waters. Cast your understanding of God's grace as your sufficiency upon the waters. Cast your realization of God as all good upon the waters, and it will return to you. Yes, we must be in the world but not of it. We must take care of our business, of our family life, of our social life, of our community life, of our national life, and our international life, but we must not accept the world's standards of what is taking place.

We, above all, even while watching the passing parade of human events, must stand back and realize that inherent in this world is no power of evil. Even with the eyes closed, we look out upon this world and realize that no one and nothing in this universe has inherent in it a power of, or propensity for, evil. We make this a daily practice, if necessary twice daily, so that always we come to the altar of prayer with no enmity in our consciousness, that is, no belief in an evil power, an evil presence, an evil condition, or an evil potentiality. In that attitude our prayer reaches the throne of heaven; it reaches the very center of our being, and good flows and permeates our entire universe.

To God we give a purified consciousness, purified with the understanding that God alone is good, that God's goodness is the goodness of individual being, individual condition, thought, and thing. Nothing else is power; nothing else is law. We behold the Christ sitting behind the eyes of every individual. We behold the Christ as the substance and law of every condition, and then there is no duality in our consciousness, and no duality can return unto us. We are the masters of our fate, the captains of our own souls in proportion to the truth that we know. "Ye shall know the truth, and the truth shall make you free."[8] It is *we* who are captains of our soul and masters of our fate by the degree of the truth that we know.

No Opposition to Truth

There is only one truth; that truth is God. To behold evil is to behold evil in God, because of God, or in spite of God. An infinity of good, an eternality of good, the all good is the only truth.

> Purge my consciousness of the belief
> in two powers. Purge my consciousness
> of the belief in appearances that would testify
> to a good power or an evil power.
> Purge my consciousness so that I know there is no
> power other than God, infinite good.

Nothing in all this world opposes two times two being four. Nothing opposes the value of do, re, mi, fa, so, la, ti, do. These are maintained and sustained unto eternity without any opposition because there is no evil to destroy the fourness of two times two or the do, re, mi-ness of do, re, mi. These qualities and quantities are eternally intact without opposition and so are we. There is no power on earth to destroy the perfection and harmony of our being.

It is only a dual mind that has permitted us to believe in two powers. Now in this day, in this experience of God, we return to our Father's house, to our Father's consciousness where we see as God sees. Because we behold with God-consciousness, with Christ-awareness, we are too pure to behold iniquity. We do not believe that in all this universe there is an evil condition, an evil power, or an evil propensity. We are too pure. We have the mind that was in Christ Jesus and we behold what that mind saw when it said to the impotent man "Rise, take up thy bed, and walk."[9] That mind saw no condition apart from God. It saw no evil in the universe. It didn't even believe there was a good body or a bad body: there was only a God-body. The only goodness of body is God. Nobody has goodness of himself any more than a person has evil, but everyone has Godness, God-being, Christhood.

We are too pure to behold iniquity. We are too pure to behold two laws operating in this universe, a good one and a bad one. We are too pure to behold two powers, two substances, a good one and an evil one, a spiritual one and a material one. We are too pure to behold iniquity because we behold through the mind that was in Christ Jesus. We behold through the vision that God has given us, the vision shown us on the mount: one power, one presence, and that one God.

Spiritual Freedom

Why have we taken so long to meet the discords and inharmonies of human sense? Is it not because we have persisted in accepting the belief that there is someone or something to get rid of? We have been beholding a selfhood apart from God, and as long as we entertain that, we cannot be free in Christ. Never seek to be free from anything or anyone; never seek to be free from any condition because then you set up duality. Seek freedom in Christ. Never seek freedom from: seek freedom in.

I am free in Christ. Christ is my freedom.
Christ is the love that permeates my being.
Christ is the liberty wherewith I am clad.
Christ is my freedom, harmony, health, wholeness,
completeness, and perfection.
I do not seek freedom from anything.
I realize my freedom in spiritual being.
I realize my freedom in the oneness of Consciousness
in which there is no presence or power opposed to
God. My freedom is in and of Christ.
It is never from anything or anybody.

Freedom is a quality of God which we enjoy when we overcome duality, when we no longer entertain a sense of separation from God, when we no longer entertain a sense of power apart from God. Then are we free in God, clad with the liberty of the sons of God. We are clothed and in our right mind only when we are too pure to behold iniquity, when we refuse to entertain any sense of iniquity, evil, destruction, or calamity. We do not realize that as long as there is duality in individual consciousness, there will be the discords of earth. But it does not come nigh the dwelling place of the "he that dwelleth in the secret place of the most High,"[10] the he who is too pure to behold iniquity, acknowledge it, or agree that it is so.

No man is a healer, and no man can become a healer, but every man can be a revealer of God's grace and God's harmony, God's peace permeating his universe. This appears to outer sense as healing but in just the same way that the mathematician corrects the belief that two times two is five with the understanding that two times two is four. He didn't bring about a healing because two times two was never other than four, so he corrected nothing. He changed nothing except a belief and an erroneous premise. So with us, we never heal but we correct the belief that there is something to be healed, that there are two powers operating in human experience.

Contemplating Truth

We become so pure, so single-minded that we acknowledge God's law alone operative in all of God's creation. The contemplation of this truth is a contemplative form of meditation. It is a contemplation of spiritual truth, but it is more than this. It is a communion with truth and in truth, and it is prayer as well as treatment. It can be called by any of these names. Actually the highest name we can give to it is contemplative meditation because when we are in meditation, we have withdrawn from the world. We have shut the world out from our eyes and ears so that inwardly we can meditate and in our meditation contemplate truth, the nature of truth as One, so that actually there is no such thing as a lie.

In the contemplation of truth as power there is no such thing as evil power. We contemplate truth as substance so that there is no substance to be destroyed or removed. We contemplate God's grace and God's goodness, and this contemplating in meditation results in the prayer of realization. It is a prayer that comes to a realization in which that which we have been contemplating automatically becomes real and demonstrable within us.

After our contemplation we have our few moments of complete silence in which we say to the Father, "Speak, Lord; for thy servant heareth,"[11] and then we wait until an assurance comes within us, a feeling that this that we have declared is true. This is the truth that we have realized, and up from within our own being there comes to us the assurance of God's presence and of God being on the field.

A meditation may not bring out what is called healing, nor

may prayer. Treatment may not bring it out either unless you are lifted to the point of realization. So when you have meditated, contemplated, when you have prayed or treated, do not be satisfied, but sit back, relax, turn to the Father within, and then listen and wait for the seal to be placed upon your prayer or meditation.

Pure Contemplation

A contemplative meditation is one in which, without any thought of healing anybody or helping anyone, you are making contact with God. Those periods of meditation are purely for your own benefit, separate and apart from whatever work you may do for others. A contemplative prayer or meditation is your period of silence in which you contemplate God and those things that pertain to God. Such prayer may be on a thousand different subjects.

Everybody knows what health is from a physical standpoint: the heart beating rhythmically, the pulse beating so many beats per minute, the blood pressure within a certain range, the digestion and elimination functioning normally. All of that constitutes health according to physical standards, but that is not spiritual wholeness because spiritual wholeness is not of this world. The spiritual kingdom is not physical: it is spiritual.

The day comes on this path when you go beyond trying to demonstrate things and you become a little curious. You are no longer interested too much in just having a physical healing. Now you come to the place where you are seeking your demonstration of eternal health, and that is when you go into contemplative meditation and turn to the Father with a question:

Father, looking out from
Your eyes, what is health?
What is the spiritual sense of health?
What is health when it really is eternality and

immortality? What is health when the body
is no longer acting or reacting under the law but
comes under grace?
What would I be experiencing of health
if I were living under grace and
if I were not under the law of matter,
medicine, food, climate, age, or decomposition?

As you contemplate the spiritual sense of health, eventually you come to the place where you say, "'Speak, Lord; for thy servant heareth.'[12] I am through. Now it is Your turn." Then you sit in that silence and in that expectant attitude. Whether it is that day, the next, or some other day, eventually you are going to get the answer to what spiritual health is.

Another day in your contemplative meditation, you might take wealth, abundance, or supply as the subject because, according to human standards, you know what that is, but you have no idea at all what spiritual abundance, spiritual supply, or spiritual substance is. In your contemplation, you will go to the Father:

What is the bread of life?
What is that meat that the Master spoke about?
What is the wine of inspiration?
What is the water that springs up into life eternal?
What is spiritual supply, spiritual food?
What is their inner esoteric meaning?
What did Jesus have in mind when he said those
things? What did Paul mean when he said,
"My grace is sufficient for thee?"[13] What is grace?
What does grace have to do with supply?

In such an earnest, quiet, peaceful contemplation, you are praying. It is a different form of prayer, but it is praying. You are turning to God and seeking knowledge from God; you are asking; you are knocking; you are seeking to be taught of God. You are not asking for a parking space and you are not seeking a new automobile and you are not knocking for a new house. But when you turn within as the Master taught, not for food, drink, or clothing, but seek, ask, and knock for spiritual light, for spiritual enlightenment, for spiritual wisdom, then you can meditate:

Father, what is supply spiritually?
What is Thy grace that should be my sufficiency?
It is a beautiful quotation,
but I would like to prove it. How can I if I don't
know what it means.
What does it mean? Thy grace is my sufficiency.
What does it mean to live by grace?
What does it mean to come out from under the law,
be separate, and live under grace?

Do Not Be Hasty to Give Truth to the World

Keep what is revealed to you as something sacred and secret until the time when it is such a positive conviction and realization that you are able to demonstrate it in bringing forth harmony in your experience and that of those around you. Then, and then only, can you begin to teach it to others.

This appearance-world is forever testifying to the pairs of opposites, life and death, sickness and health, abundance and lack. These appearances have registered themselves so deeply upon us that many find it hard to believe that there is nobody and nothing in all of this universe that has an evil power, propensity, or capacity. Yet it is so. But it is a highly evolved realization that comes only through spiritual discernment, inner reflection, pondering, meditation. This is the highest revelation given in the Master's teaching, a revelation which only a few of his disciples were able to grasp. It has been lost to the world because of its depth and because of appearances it is almost impossible to accept. One of these days the truth of the non-power of appearances will be revealed to you from within your own being. At this moment some of you have only my word for it or a few passages of scripture. Some of you are a step further and have an inner feeling that what you are reading is true. But none of this is enough. As Mary took the babe down to Egypt to hide it for a year, so must you take this gem into your consciousness, hide it, ponder it, and meditate upon it until the day comes when something within you says it is true.

Treasure these truths within yourself as you would cherish gems and then share them discreetly with those who are appreciative of them. For I give it unto you that the evidence of the senses tells us that sin, disease, and lack have power within themselves detrimental to us. I give it to you as a spiritual truth that there is no power either of good or evil in anything or anyone. All power is God and that power is good.

Now you will be able to understand the Master when he says, "My peace give I unto you."[14] In that consciousness of his which was too pure to behold evil, he saw no evil to be overcome, he saw no disease to be healed, he saw no sin from which to be reformed. He beheld a spiritual universe filled with God's grace and was able to say, "My peace—my consciousness, which is not divided against itself, but which is of the household of God, having in it only children of God, the peace of God—give I unto you." As you can entertain within yourselves this divine idea, this spiritual truth of Oneness, you will find that the power of the Christ-peace of an undivided household will descend upon you.

Chapter Six

The Discipline of Knowing the Truth

Students of the Infinite Way are taught to go into prayer, treatment, or a contemplative healing meditation without words, opening their consciousness in a state of receptivity, listening for that "still small voice,"[1] and letting It give the treatment and do the work. On the other hand, students are taught to know the truth, declare the truth, remind themselves of truth, and go through a degree of mental discipline. Unless students understand these two approaches clearly, there might seem to be a conflict or a contradiction. But there is no conflict or contradiction.

Spiritual Preparation Needed

In the early stages of the development of spiritual consciousness, it is necessary to go through disciplines: mental disciplines, specific practice, and many forms of work that will not be used or be necessary later. In our earliest study, we fill ourselves full of truth through books, lectures, classes, or in any way in which truth can be imbibed. We spend hours and hours a day in reading, studying, meditating. We spend weeks, sometimes months, years attending classes, and we know the truth specifically about many things, probably about everything that touches our human experience.

In doing that, let us understand that we are not doing it for the sake of God, nor are we doing it to reach God or to get something from God. As a matter of fact, such practices have very little to do with God: they have to do with preparing ourselves and making us fit for the receptivity to God. By that, I do not mean humanly fit or humanly good, but making ourselves spiritually receptive. That is what takes the preparation.

Different Approaches Lead to God

The more we read inspired literature, correct metaphysical or spiritual literature, and fill ourselves with it, the more our thought becomes spiritualized and the clearer transparencies we become. True, too, the more inspirational lectures to which we listen and the more classes we attend, the more we are spiritualizing ourselves. This does not mean selecting indiscriminately classes or teachers, but praying to be led to the book, approach, teaching, or teacher most akin to our state of consciousness, and then following that line as long as it appears to be our way.

I find as much fault with persons who run from lecture to lecture or teacher to teacher indiscriminately as I do with those who constantly run to theaters or movies without wisely selecting what they are going to see or with those who buy books indiscriminately. In our progressive unfoldment, there is certain reading that is right for you and for me. To such reading we should be led and then follow it.

There are persons who must approach the study and search for God from a purely emotional standpoint. Never doubt for a moment that they can reach It that way, at least many of them. Those persons will find great satisfaction in such church services as are found in the Episcopalian Church, the Catholic Church, or the Hebrew Temple, where the emotions are aroused and where a deep appeal is made to the senses. There are those who find their way to God in just that way.

There are others who could never reach God using that approach, and they would have to reach It more from the standpoint of reason and intellect by thinking things through. Those persons come by way of the mental sciences where the human mind is the factor and where emphasis is placed on human cause and effect. Although that approach may be only an initial step leading to something higher, it may be necessary for those who are thus conditioned to find their way mentally.

There are still others who cannot find their way through either of those approaches and who will find it only through the purely spiritual way, only through direct contact with God, through inspirational literature which is uplifting and elevating. That type of person is the one who feels especially comfortable with the Infinite Way because the Infinite Way is primarily an attempt to lift consciousness and maintain it on a level where the individual can realize a direct contact with God. The spiritual approach does not claim to make the contact for us, but through its inspirational writing and consciousness it does raise us to the place where we ourselves are able to make that contact.

Knowing the Truth

Regardless of the approach through which we may come, there are always certain disciplines. There is work to be done, and this is true in the Infinite Way. No matter how spiritual the approach and no matter how close to God we come, there are those periods when it becomes necessary to lift ourselves into an atmosphere of God and to raise ourselves up from the level to which we have sunk through radio, newspaper, gossip, and all the things that happen to us out here in the world. They all have the effect of pulling us down, and it sometimes takes a great deal of reading, a considerable amount of meditation, or association with those on the path, to lift us up again. Above all, the place the discipline has is that through it we actually know what the truth is so we do not have a blind faith in an unknown God. Even if a blind faith demonstrates something for us temporarily, it is not a good place to be because sooner or later it fails us. There must be an actual knowing of what the truth is and of making it so much a part of our being that there is no possibility of our forgetting it in a time of trouble.

Meeting World-Suggestion with Truth

The truth that *I,* at the center of my being, which is God, the divine Consciousness, is really the substance, the law, and the activity of my universe is contradicted a hundred times a day out here in life. A hundred times a day something tells us that we need money, we need food, we need clothing, or we are in danger from bombs or war. Constantly the argument is presented to us contradicting the basic truth that our consciousness is the "secret place of the most High,"[2] that our own consciousness is our security and safety, and that there is nothing outside us that can enter to defile or make a lie. Not even an atomic bomb can reach us once we have learned the truth that our consciousness is the fortress, the rock, "the secret place of the most High." Because we are abiding in that secret place, nothing out here can come in to injure, mislead, misguide, misdirect, harm, or deprive us of anything in life.

A thousand times a day we are told where we should go for safety, security, and protection, and each time that suggestion is thrown at us we must come back within ourselves with the answer that safety and security are not found outside. Safety and security are found only in "the secret place of the most High," in the temple of God within our own being, within our consciousness.

It sounds foolish and decidedly impractical to the human mind to believe that this consciousness right here where we are is a protection from germs and bombs outside, and yet that is the truth of scripture. In the 23rd, 27th, and 91st Psalms and all through scripture, it is brought out that if we dwell in the consciousness of God forever, none of these things can come nigh our dwelling place.

Resting in the Assurance of God's Presence

When faced with an overwhelming enemy, Hezekiah exhorted his people: "Be strong and courageous, be not afraid nor dismayed for the king of Assyria, nor for all the multitude that is with him: for there be more with us than with him: With him is an arm of flesh; but with us is the Lord our God to help us, . . . And the people rested themselves upon the words of Hezekiah."[3] That is a strange sounding message, isn't it? We might think they would have rested themselves on Hezekiah's armies, defenses, and ammunition. No, they rested themselves on the words of Hezekiah, and those words were that the enemy was just "an arm of flesh," whereas they had the Lord God almighty, and they were resting in that assurance.

We, too, are taught to rest, but to rest in the word of scripture. As long as we abide in the word of God and let the word of God abide in us, we are in that sacred place of the most High, in divine Consciousness where nothing enters to harm or disturb.

Even when we have agreed that this is the truth, it will be only a few hours after we are thus established before we may be tempted into disbelieving and distrusting it. Just hearing a radio newscast or glancing at a newspaper headline, and out the window goes all of this truth, that is, unless we are alert and willing to discipline ourselves to answer every suggestion, every rumor, and every appearance of evil with a conscious rebuke: Where do we place our trust? Is our trust in something visible or tangible, or is it in the Invisible, in that which the world cannot see, hear, taste, touch, or smell but which we know exists? Is our trust in the divine Consciousness, God, the soul of us at the center of our being, in that which makes it possible to realize that the place whereon we stand is holy ground? What makes this place holy ground? Is it not the truth that *I*, the divine Consciousness, enfolds us and holds us within Its embrace? Even though we cannot physically see It out there, those of spiritual discernment are aware of It.

To some that *I* appears as light. Often people in audiences tell me that they have seen light. I do not see It as a light myself very often, but I feel It almost like a cloud, a beautiful cloud in the sky that is right around me, and I can lean back on It and feel It. It is as real and tangible to me as if It were a steel suit of armor, only It is soft and gentle, but I know that bullets or bombs cannot penetrate it.

Seeing Through the Appearance

At our present state of development, it is necessary to recognize that all evil is presented to us as suggestion or appearance. One day we may pick up the paper, listen to the radio, or hear our neighbor tell how many polio cases there are. That is a suggestion thrust upon us to believe in some evil outside our own being. We have to see through that. Another day, it may be the war scare, another day the political situation, and yet another day, the economic problem. Whatever it is, we must be alert to remember it is being presented to us as a suggestion, an argument, or an appearance, and we are called on to do something about it. What we are called on to do about it is to see through it.

Such a response has nothing to do with God. It has nothing to do with prayer in its highest sense. It has to do with prayer in its lower sense, and we call that treatment or contemplative meditation. Treatment is a form of prayer, and not a very high form, because it is not really a direct approach to God. Treatment is really the preparation of our mind so that the truth of God may enter. By means of treatment, the practitioner lifts himself in consciousness to where he can then listen and be receptive to God.

It may well be that with some appearances of error, the practitioner, because of the press of circumstances, may not be able to stand fast in not accepting them. Then the practitioner would be wise to stop all outer activity to bring to conscious awareness some truth: "Now wait a minute. What is this coming at me? It is an appearance. Do I have to believe it? No, why should I believe anything apart from God? God created all that was made, and all that God made is good, and anything God did not make was not made. And so if it is not good, this thing never was made. It has no reality; it has no substance, law, cause, or effect. Therefore, I do not have to accept it into my consciousness or believe it."

This has nothing to do with God; it has to do with the practitioner. All the practitioner has done is clear his mind of the appearance. When that has been done, the practitioner can put the finger on the lips and become very still, and in a listening state he is making his conscious contact with God, opening consciousness to a receptivity to truth.

Only when we open our consciousness to God is God made available to us. In that silence, the final part of the treatment, we are still until we have the assurance of God's presence. Once we know God is on the field, we are not concerned anymore about the case or the patient. Now it is with God.

Rising Above Fear or Faith in the Visible

Before we develop the spiritual consciousness that is open and receptive to God, there is spade work to be done, and that spade work consists of refuting the appearances and suggestions and knowing the basic truth. Until we become convinced that the real power of the world is within our own being, we will be under the necessity of mentally disciplining ourselves every time we come up against an appearance contrary to that. Thus we will be building or unfolding our spiritual consciousness.

Spiritual consciousness is our consciousness when our complete faith is in the Invisible. Material consciousness exists as long as we have a faith in, or fear of, something in the visible. How long will it take us to overcome our faith in, or fear of, that which is in the external? No one knows. That is a matter that we individually demonstrate. Some of us must work weeks, months, and even years before we reach a state of consciousness in which nothing in the external world is of so great value that we will do much about getting it, and nothing in the external world is so much feared that we have much concern about it.

It may take a long time to come to the realization that the kingdom of God is within. The kingdom of safety, security, the kingdom of peace, the kingdom of companionship and supply—all of that is within us. That is what I mean by mental discipline, by a knowing of specific truth:

Consciousness at the center of my being
is the substance, the law,
and the activity unto everything
that appears in my universe.

Consciousness Draws Unto Itself Its Own

If you are my friend, it is only because the divine Consciousness at the center of my being has empowered us to become friends. If you are drawn to this work, it is because your consciousness has become the law, the substance, and the activity drawing that work to you. I draw my own to me, and you are drawn to your own. The soul at the center of you and the soul at the center of me draw together all those equipped to be receptive to this level of consciousness. It also forces out those not a part of this activity or of our consciousness. Jesus "came unto his own."[4] "My sheep hear my voice, and I know them, and they follow me."[5]

There must be something at the center of my consciousness

drawing unto me my own. So, too, there is something at the center of your consciousness drawing to you the very books you need, the very teacher, the very teaching, and the wherewithal to get it and enjoy it. That is all taking place at the center of your own consciousness. If you are looking outside for books, teachers, or money to get them, you are looking in the wrong place, and even if you get them they will not be right for you. If, however, you turn within and realize that this Consciousness, Soul, or Spirit, your soul at the very center of your being, is the substance of your world and It creates your world for you, a world of harmony, wholeness, completeness, and perfection, that is spiritual consciousness. The developing of that spiritual consciousness, however, depends on your effort, on the effort that you put in continuously reminding yourself:

My soul is the substance of my world.
My soul is the substance of my supply.
My soul is even the nourishing
value of the food I eat.
My soul imparts to
the food I eat Its nourishment.
My soul, spirit, or consciousness imparts
the power of friendship in the world.

It takes a good bit of discipline to keep reminding yourself of the truth:

Within me is the kingdom of God.
Within me is the substance and
the activity of life.
Right within my own being is all that
is necessary to bring me a life of
harmony, peace, joy, power, and dominion.
The kingdom of God is within me.

So there are two stages that seem to conflict, one in which we vigorously know the truth every time there is an appearance or suggestion opposing it, and then that part of the teaching which says you do not have to know the truth at all. It is God that knows the truth. When throughout your day you have reminded yourself of the truth of being, when you have withdrawn from the world the power to harm you, the power to hurt you, the power to make you ill or poor, and have realized that the entire power of the universe is within your own being, then when you sit down to work out some specific problem for yourself or another, you are in the position to engage in that higher form of prayer that is wordless and thoughtless. You do not need a word or a thought in that prayer.

God Can Define Itself to You in Many Ways

When you sit down to meditate, having first eliminated any fear of appearances, you are ready for the supreme experience of meeting God face to face. Some persons have experienced God through the sense of smell. They have actually smelled the perfume of beautiful flowers all around them when there was none. That was the spiritual atmosphere of God which was appearing to them in the form of fragrance. Some have a sense of meeting God face to face in inspiring music, melodies that have never been put on paper or played by any instrument. There are others who meet God face to face through just a feeling of God's presence, through God defining Itself in that way.

There is no use in outlining how you will meet God face to face, but you will be aware of God when you attain that higher sense of prayer. To reach that higher sense of prayer it must be recognized that some discipline may be required. It may be that when you first sit down for this purpose, nothing seems to happen. You do not get any feeling; in fact, nothing comes. Do not be concerned about it, but as you continue this practice over the weeks and months, gradually there will be a conscious awareness of the Presence in one form or another. Do not become discouraged. It will not elude you forever. You will experience It; you will feel It; but *when* depends largely on your background and on the degree of your dedication.

My first experience with meditation came as a result of a realization that meditation was the way of life for me. I also realized I knew nothing about meditation. So I tried to meditate. It took me eight months. I practiced never less than twenty times a day, anywhere from two to five or ten minutes at a time, never less than twenty times a day and for eight months. In all that time I had no response. Nothing at all seemed to be happening. It was just as if I had wasted two, three, five, six, or seven minutes. But I was determined to keep it up.

For years I have lived from day to day and week to week, one year following another, with no change taking place. Nothing happened. Something had to be introduced that was not there before, and not knowing of any other way, I was determined to try meditation. So I stuck with it for eight months, but at the end of eight months I had my reward in the first experience of the tiniest flash—far less than a second—of something happening. I could not tell whether it was a flash of light I had seen or the flash of the Presence going by, but something happened in that second that gave me encouragement to go on.

From there on it progressed slowly, very slowly. Probably once in a day or once in three or four days, something would happen to make me feel I was on the right track. That went on for a long time until gradually the time came whenever I sat down to meditate I could be assured that before I finished the meditation there would be a feeling of the Presence. If nothing else, there might be just a deep sigh, a release from whatever was bothering me, and all was well.

Remarkable changes took place in the outer world as the Presence became a living experience. My mode of life did not change immediately. I kept on in the same pattern with the exception of the meditations, but I can assure you that I kept the meditation going. Then that meditation, evidently acting as the Presence going before me to "make the crooked places straight,"[6] began transforming the outer world. It brought supply and opportunities to me that seemed to come out of a clear sky. By that time, however, I had learned that there was nothing that comes out of a clear sky. It comes for a very definite reason and it comes from a very definite place, out of the depths of your own consciousness. You have to reach a depth within your consciousness that releases the power to go out into the world to do whatever is necessary for you.

Practice Is Essential

The Presence does go before you, and It "makes the crooked places straight"—if you have the conscious awareness of the Presence. There are persons all over the world declaring, "The Presence goes before me," and It does not do a single thing for them. No, no, the Presence does not go before you just because you declare some words, nor is God consciously present with you just because you declare It.

God is an experience. God must be experienced, and we experience God through our meditation. I am not saying meditation is the only way to have the experience. There are people on earth who have never meditated who have a conscious awareness of the presence of God all the time. But those who have not had the experience of the presence of God have not lived, and if they have not experienced the presence of God, it is because they have not specifically known the truth and then gone to the source where God is to be found.

Do you understand now what I mean when I point out there must be discipline and a declaration or statement of truth, a realization of truth, and yet, in the same breath, I say that when you get to the point of prayer or treatment, you do not need words or thoughts? Lets this be clear to you. Do not hesitate about it, because it is very important. I have had persons say that there is no use telling Mr. Goldsmith about their troubles; he won't do anything about them. They get that idea because I will not sit back and talk about them for a long while or go over all the details with them. I do plenty about them, but I do not always do it in the way they think it should be done. Other people say that Mr. Goldsmith does not give treatments. That is not true either.

The Infinite Way Is Not an Absolute Teaching

There are persons who think Mr. Goldsmith is absolute. He is not. Never believe it. Nobody is absolute who resorts to treatment, books, words, lectures, or classes. Any time anyone goes further than saying, "I Am," he is no longer absolute, because everything else exists in the relative. Every time I am faced with appearances in the outer world, I consciously remember:

The center of my being is my sanctuary.
The center of my being
is the place where God abides.
The center of God's being is where I abide,
and that is right here where I am,
since I and the Father are one.

Every time I am faced with an outside appearance, I am not absolute about it at all. I have a realization within myself:

I and the Father are one,
and all that the Father has is mine,
right here where I am now.
The soul of my being is the substance of
what I am eating.
Everything that goes into my system

must partake of the nature
of my own soul, spirit, or consciousness.
It is the very activity of God within me that
is the value of the food I eat.

The soul of my being is the value
of whatever money I receive;
and it is the value of whatever money I give out.
The soul at the center of my being is
the value unto my supply.
The soul at the center of my being
is the law unto this body.

I never am so absolute that I do not remember such truths. I do not think a day goes by that I do not consciously remember sometime or other:

God at the center of me, the soul of me,
is the substance, the life, and the activity of this body,
of its organs and its functions,
and that is why this body is immortal.
This body is vital and alive for
the simple reason that God is the substance of it,
God is the activity of it, and God is the only law
unto it. No calendar is a law unto it,
and neither are food, vitamins, calories, or germs.

God animates, feeds, supplies, maintains,
and sustains my being, that very God of my being
which is my soul, my spirit, my consciousness.
That which is the reality of my being is the law unto
my mind, unto my soul, unto my purse,
unto my body, unto my universe,
unto my practice, unto my student body.
God is the substance of it and,

if God is not the substance of my practice
and my student body, I would not want it even
though it might be humanly profitable.
I want only that part of the practice or
that part of the student body which is a part
of my household, of my consciousness,
that which is of God.

While everything and everyone is of God, there are states and stages of consciousness, and those persons who are not a part of this particular state of consciousness must gravitate to that place and that teacher and that teaching where they can be blessed. Their purpose in life is to find their teacher. My purpose in life is to find my own students so that we all can be of one household, of one state of consciousness. The absolute aspect of the Infinite Way and of prayer in the healing work is that this truth is so deeply ingrained in me that if you present a problem to me I may not have to go over all that ground specifically and declare the truth every time you call or every time there are a dozen calls. Now it may be necessary only to sit down, get still, and in a minute or two or three or five, that feeling of God's presence comes and the work is done.

There are times, however, when I have to sit up all night to meet a case. There are times when I may have to work for days to pull a case through that seems to be slipping out for the simple reason that the only time we meet these so-called desperate cases is when we reach an elevation of consciousness that meets the need. Our work in the Infinite Way is not an attempt to be absolute. It is not an attempt to set ourselves up on some high cloud only to be knocked off some sweet day.

No God And

We are not absolute in this work except in our realization of God as the absolute infinite All. There we take our stand in the absolute that there is not God *and.* There is not God *and* a universe. There is not God *and* man. There is not God *and* good. Since God is infinite, God is all; and that Infinity may appear as you, as me, and as a billion others, but it is still that one Infinity appearing.

A person can have all of everything spiritual and not deprive anyone else of that allness. We can have all of life—infinite, eternal, and immortal life. Every one of us can have that and not deprive his neighbor of a bit of it. Why is that true? Because there are not lives many: there is one Life fulfilling Itself as your life and as my life. In that way we are absolute. There is not God *and* you. There is God manifesting Itself, the Word becoming flesh. There is not the Word *and* flesh: there is the Word which becomes flesh and appears individually as you and as me, but it is still the Word. So there is God, infinite God, manifesting Its life as my life and as your life, manifesting Its mind as my mind and as your mind, Its soul as my soul and as your soul. There is not God-Soul and my soul or your soul: there is God-Soul individualized or appearing as my soul and as your soul, only one. In that awareness we are absolute.

Chapter Seven

"Where the Spirit of the Lord Is, There Is Liberty"

In meeting some of our Infinite Way students, as well as students of other teachings around the world, it puzzles me to learn from them that they feel they have a very deep understanding of truth. It is something I have never had, and something I would not know how to set about obtaining. But I meet people all the time who claim to have it, and I wonder sometimes what they do with it.

The function of the Infinite Way is not to confer on anybody a great understanding of truth, otherwise I would never have been elected and appointed by the powers that be to conduct this work. Every class that has been conducted has been without any knowledge on my part of what was to come through. I had no understanding; I had no depth of wisdom that I was going to teach or impart. I was under orders and when I went before a class, in each case whatever was to come out came out, and we now have it on tapes or in book form.

The Simplicity of Truth

The Infinite Way approach to life and to truth is to hold ourselves empty of knowledge and empty of understanding. To fill oneself with understanding and knowledge is virtually to rule out God. There is no room for God in a mind that is already filled with yesterday's manna and with knowledge that is written in books.

It has been said that knowledge is power, but since we do not need or want any power, we do not need great quantities of knowledge. We do not strive for power over one another. We do not want power over sin, disease, or death. It was on that very point that the Master cautioned the disciples: "In this rejoice not, that the spirits are subject unto you; but rather rejoice, because your names are written in heaven."[1] That is the basis of the Infinite Way.

We do not go around wielding power. We live in a constant state of gratitude that our "names are written in heaven," that in our true being we are spiritual. We may not be showing as much forth to the world as we should, but basically we know that we are not evil, that we have no evil motives or intentions. We know that we are not even as human as we appear to be in our conduct. We know we are better than that.

At the moment we have not achieved the ability to be all that we really know we are. There is not any one of us who is not far greater spiritually than is being shown forth. The proof of that truth is that even today our life is a struggle to be less human and to be more spiritual in our mode of living, conduct, and thinking. Inherently, we know our true identity is Christhood, although we know we are not living up to that standard in our human experience. We also know the only reason we are on a spiritual path is because, having recognized our spiritual identity, we seek to live up to a higher degree of that Christhood which is our true identity.

There is no great understanding or great wisdom that is going to help you or me, or any of our students to accomplish this. Truth itself is very simple. Unless we become as a child we will never know truth, because it is not given to the wise man to know truth. "The things of the spirit of God. . . are foolishness unto [the natural man],"[2] and wise men are often fools in the sight of God. Truth, if it is truth, is so simple that if it cannot be explained to a child, we can be sure it is not truth, but some man-made wisdom.

The Spirit Realized Reveals Harmony

What have we realized of truth in all these years that we have been on the path? Years of witnessing the demonstration of spiritual principles have proved the truth of the Bible passage: "Where the Spirit of the Lord is, there is liberty."[3] That is not a very profound truth, and it does not take a learned man to grasp that. Simple people, uneducated people, even very young people can grasp the idea that "where the Spirit of the Lord is, there is liberty." Nevertheless, profound scholars are devoting themselves to discovering the reason for evil on earth. People are going through years and years of study trying to find where evil comes from, trying to account for it, and here in one simple verse the answer to the whole of error is given: "Where the Spirit of the Lord is, there is liberty," but where the spirit of the Lord is not, there is error. That is how simple it is, and furthermore, it is demonstrable.

Every one of our students who has been the instrument through which any healing work has been accomplished has proved that the Spirit realized is the dissolution of any evil. Let a sick, poor, or sinful person come to one of our students for help, earnestly and sincerely desiring it, and this student would more than likely respond, "Certainly, I'll be happy to help you," and then sit down and meditate. There would be no profound discussion of truth. There would be no psychological attempt to reform the patient, tell him how loving he must be, how grateful, how pure, how much reading he must do, or any attempt to spend hours with the patient teaching him the deep wisdoms of the world. Instead, there might be just a simple statement of truth, and then the student would sit back and meditate. For what purpose? What takes place in that meditation? As quickly as possible, the student gets to the center of his own being and makes contact with that which we call God, the spirit of God in man.

There is a spirit in man. "The spirit of God hath made me, and the breath of the Almighty hath given me life."[4] There is a spirit in man that gives him peace and rest. Our function is to make conscious contact with that spirit. When we make that contact, the patient usually feels better, has relief, a complete healing takes place, is offered employment or is comforted. Something of a very positive nature happens as a result of the meditation. If a complete healing has not been achieved, the student repeats the process as many times as he is called upon by the patient or student until the meditations do their work.

The student of himself has done nothing except the hardest work there is in all the world, and that is to put aside any sense of self, of one's own understanding, one's power, or one's ego, so as to make contact with that invisible Spirit, and let It have Its way. Where misunderstandings arise and where patients sometimes become dissatisfied with the results is when the patient does not always understand the nature and purpose of the meditations, the treatment, the work, or the function of the Infinite Way.

The Spirit of God Realized Penetrates the Veils that Hide Reality

Through the reading of metaphysical literature or accepting somebody's promises, patients may believe that it is our function to heal their diseases, to prevent their sins, to see that they get profitable employment, or are blessed with an abundance of the world's goods. Far be that from the purpose of the Infinite Way. As human beings, each of us has material blocks keeping us from experiencing God's grace, and the purpose of our work is to remove those blocks. That is what happens in a meditation. When the spirit of God comes, It does not remove our disease, sin, or poverty. What It does is to remove the materialistic block that is preventing our enjoying the fullness of the Godhead bodily.

The material sense of life, the one into which we were born and brought up, is devoted entirely to the glorification of our personal selfhood. Its goal is to get all the money we think we need, the name, fame, or health. In other words, it is a catering to our personal selfhood. That is all that material existence consists of, a continuous catering to the little self. When we improve and become a little better, we begin being good to our mothers and fathers and children, and we really believe that that is being spiritual. By the time that we are able to be good to our cousins, nephews, and nieces, we really think we are good spiritual people. All of that is nonsense.

"Pray for them which despitefully use you, and persecute you; . . . For if ye love them which love you, what reward have ye?"[5] It profits a man nothing to be good to his parents, his children, his friends, even to his cousins and fellow Republicans or Democrats. It becomes a spiritual way of life when we can pray that God's grace illumine human consciousness, whether it be our friends or our enemies, our relatives or your relatives. It becomes a spiritual activity when we are willing for the sinners of the world to be forgiven their sins. Whether or not we can forgive them is of relative unimportance. What counts is that we be willing that God's forgiveness and God's grace touch them.

The function of our meditation is, first of all, to purify ourselves of self: selfishness, self-righteousness, ego, jingoistic patriotism, all these things in which crimes are committed. Furthermore, our meditations are to eliminate or to dissipate personal sense in the patient or student who comes to us, to dissolve the grosser elements that make up material or human living. When these changes have taken place in consciousness so that we become softer, more mellow, less demanding, more forgiving, more generous, not merely in the sense of giving more dollars, but in the wider circle to which we give those dollars, the sins of the body, the diseases and the lacks of the body begin to disappear.

It often does happen that a person comes to a spiritual healer for help and receives that help without any immediate sign of a change in his disposition or character taking place. Actually, that is not true. If we watch that person over the next few years, it is usually evident that a change has taken place in him, and unless it has he may revert to his previous condition. The Master covered that situation when he said, "Neither do I condemn thee; go, and sin no more."[6] We have observed in our work that many times people have come to us for physical healings and received them with no apparent change occurring in their spiritual or moral fibre, and then shortly afterwards either reverted to the same disease or something just as bad, and sometimes worse. In other words, they benefited from the degree of consciousness of their practitioner, but they could not hold on to that benefit. They went back to their grossness, their materiality, or their selfishness and lapsed into whatever the discords were.

The Spirit Sets Us Free from the Personal Sense of Life

"Where the Spirit of the Lord is, there is liberty." If, through our meditation, we can bring to a person's consciousness the spirit of the Lord, that spirit will free the person from material sense and from various forms of ego. All forms of ego are not humanly bad. Some are humanly very good. Spiritually, however, they are destructive.

Sometimes mother love is as destructive to the child as mother hate would be, because it is not love at all. It is very often a human sense of love that would protect the child from all the discords, inharmonies, trials, and tribulations of life. Then, when the child goes out into the world and is not prepared for what he has to face in the world, he begins to realize that some of that love was not real love at all. In some cases I have witnessed parents sending their children to college and being sure that all their bills were paid and that they did not have to work or earn any part of their expenses and then I have seen how the children became devoid of initiative because when they came out of school they were so accustomed to having everything done for them that they never engaged in any really constructive activity. The parents thought they were making sacrifices for the child: what they were doing was sacrificing the child.

"Where the Spirit of the Lord is, there is liberty." When an individual has in some measure risen above the personal sense of life, that is, is no longer living for his own sake, just making money for himself, for his family, for personal gain or personal fame, or for any personal reason, but has come to a state of consciousness where he is devoting himself even in a measure, to the stranger, the wayfarer, the seeker, that individual is able to bring to light the spirit of God. The greater the degree of a person's own rising above the personal sense of life, the greater degree of the spirit of God does such a one bring into experience. The Master illustrated that, first of all in saying, "He that loseth his life for my sake shall find it,"[7] indicating that in order to gain our life we must lose it. He, himself, was willing to lose and sacrifice the physical sense of life for what he thought or believed was to be his demonstration of immortality, the example that was to set the world free.

It makes no difference whether he succeeded in convincing many people at that moment or whether there have been many or few convinced since then. It is true that ultimately "every knee shall bow to me,"[8] every knee will bend to that experience of the crucifixion, and everyone will see that the life of Jesus Christ was not forfeit, but that in forfeiting his *physical sense* of life he demonstrated the supreme function of brotherly love and immortality.

It is not a profound or deep understanding or knowledge of truth that makes such a demonstration. It is the simple understanding that whenever the spirit of the Lord can be made evident, victory, immortality, health, harmony, wholeness, completeness, and perfection can be made evident. It would really make no difference if a person were on a battlefield, in the midst of a depression, in the midst of infection or contagion, wherever there is an individual who can rise to contact with the inner Selfhood, that which we call the Christ, Spirit, or presence of God, safety is made evident, security, peace, health, harmony. Even the dead are raised in the presence of a deep enough degree of spiritual realization.

God or Truth Revealed from Within

To know the truth that makes us free is to know simple truth. It is true that we have to get away from many of the church teachings that have been presented to mankind through the ages, because it becomes necessary for an individual to become free enough in his own mind to ask the question, "What is truth?" and not ask it of "man, whose breath is in his nostrils"[9] or of men who are in high places. When he asks it of the Father within, he will then be led to the right teaching, the right teacher, or the right book.

When we come to such a book, teacher, or teaching, we discover that simplicity is the nature of the message, because that teaching will reveal, so far as possible, the nature of God. God is like nothing that we have been taught. God is not something separate and apart from our own being, but God is that which actually constitutes our being. If we ever have any hope of meeting God, we will have to meet God somewhere that is closer than any book and closer than any teacher can get us. If we really want God, we must understand that God is to be found within us. The kingdom is neither "Lo here! Or, Lo there! For, behold the kingdom of God is within you."[10] It is not in explanations; it is not in answers to questions. The nature of God is such that it cannot be defined by the human mind. It can be imparted in meditation, and it can be realized in meditation, but it cannot be defined.

To search in the realm of the human mind to understand God is nonsense. To be able to settle down within and to realize that God is not knowable by, to, or through the human mind, that God is Spirit or an awareness that reveals Itself within us, it becomes necessary to be patient, to learn to abide within ourselves and let God reveal Itself to us. There is no record that the Buddha was taught by anybody what God is, that Jesus was taught by anybody what God is, that Elijah was taught what God is, or that Moses was taught by any man what God is. To each of these persons, it was revealed within himself what God is.

And so it is with us. Nobody is going to reveal to us what God is. To be told that God is life, truth, love, or spirit is not telling us what God is. It is just giving us more words to memorize, words of which we have no knowledge. "And this is life eternal, that they might know thee the only true God."[11] Every true spiritual teacher will tell us that we must know God. Each one will tell us that the kingdom of God is within us, and that is where we must come face to face with our God or Truth. That is why there is nothing profound about truth. It is simple. The moment we begin to believe that we know it, we are allowing mere knowledge to usurp the place of God Itself. If it should come to choosing between God and knowledge, is there any choice?

Reason for Emphasis on the Nature of Error

In the Infinite Way, a great deal of attention is paid to the subject of the nature of error. There is nothing mysterious about the nature of error, but it is necessary to understand it, because regardless of what our approach to the religious life has been, regardless of what our background has been, we have accepted a universal belief that there are two powers: God and devil, God and Satan, good and evil, or immortality and mortality. We have also been taught that while actually God is the greater power and can do things to error, He very seldom does, and so we go through a life of sin, disease, lack, limitation, and wars, not that God could not stop them, but God in His inscrutable wisdom does not, which to a thinker is about as near pure nonsense as we can get.

We can be assured that if God is love, and God had the power to stop sin, disease, lack, and limitation, there would not be any on earth. As a matter of fact, God is able to stop sin, disease, lack, and limitation, and God does—in the life of everyone who realizes God, and in the life of no one else. Where the spirit of the Lord is, there is freedom. How could a man or a woman, who has realized God, continue suffering from sin, disease, lack, and the horrors of human experience.

The reason there are chapters in all of our writings and frequent references to the nature of error is to serve as a constant reminder that we must gain a conviction of God as the only power. Error is not something that we learn how to fight, battle, destroy, or to overcome through the Infinite Way. What we learn about error in the Infinite Way is that it does not exist where the spirit of the Lord is. Where individuals in their inner being achieve a realization of God's presence, the sin, disease, death, and poverty disappear. The inharmonious relationships disappear. Those with whom we come in contact either come into harmonious agreement with us, or, if they are so adamant in error, they are removed from our experience, and that is the end of them as far as we are concerned. We do not interfere with their lives, and they do not interfere with our lives anymore.

The Conscious Realization of God Removes Power from the World of Form

The simplicity of this truth is that it forever destroys idolatry in our experience. Most of the religions of the world are based on idolatry and even though they accept such passages as "Thou shalt not make unto thee any graven image. . . or bow down thyself to them,"[12] many religions continue to have images in their temples, churches, or other places of worship. When people are not worshiping them as material form, they are worshiping them as mental images, such as the devil, mortal mind, or some other form of error to which their God is supposed to do something. That is idolatry. It is idolatry to fear a germ; it is idolatry to fear infection or contagion; it is idolatry to believe that there is power in any person or any thing, including weather or climate. It is setting up an image and saying, "Oh, look what you can do to me!" If that is not idolatry, what is?

Sometimes we may believe one form of an image can do good to us, and sometimes we think it can do harm to us. If it is a good piece of pure chocolate, it can do good to us, but if it is a whole pound of it, it will do harm to us. That is idolatry. If a germ is in one form, it can be contaminating, dangerous, and destructive. If it is in another form, it can be a remedy for the same disease that in another form was destructive. There is no place where human ingenuity leaves off.

In the human picture all that is true. There is good and evil; aspirin does heal; and miracle drugs sometimes heal. In the human picture there are good climates and bad climates, but strangely enough there is no climate that is good for everybody and no climate that is harmful for everybody. Every climate can be both good and evil. There are persons in the Hawaiian Islands who are ecstatic about the wonders of the magnificent climate of this paradise of the Pacific, and then other persons up and down the Islands are suffering from the harmful influence of the weather and ultimately have to leave the Islands because the weather and climate are not right for them. That is nonsense, but in the human picture it is a fact.

What takes such power out of the human picture? The conscious realization of God is what does it—nothing else. It is the height of foolishness to go around making affirmations that food has no power, that climate, infection, contagion, and depression have no power. It is utter nonsense. They do, and as long as there is a human picture they will have power. But they have no power, they have no presence, and they do not even exist *where the spirit of the Lord is realized.*

That is why a practitioner steeped in the consciousness of one power can go into the presence of any form of sin, disease, lack, limitation, or unhappiness, and where there is a sincere and honest desire to come out of it, such practitioners must succeed, because they can bring the spirit of the Lord to bear on the situation. Their lives are dedicated; they have left so far behind self-seeking that they can bear witness to the presence of God and bring about changes in human experience. These changes come about only in proportion to the patient's willingness to accept the presence of God.

Everybody would like to get rid of disease and war. The only things people don't want to get rid of are their own qualities that perpetuate sin, disease, and war. Those they would like to hug and hold onto. Most of them would still like to go on being patriotic Americans, patriotic Japanese, patriotic Germans, and patriotic Russians, fight everybody else, and mold everybody else to their will. Almost everybody in the world wants more of the world's goods without any consideration for whom they may harm or who may suffer because of the good they are seeking. That is the human picture, a catering to personal self in all guises and disguises.

There would not be any religious warfare in the world if, for example, all the Catholics could just wipe out all the other churches and embrace us all in the loving fold of Mother Church, and I am sure that this is true of other churches, too. There would be no trouble with them if they could just wipe out the Catholics and embrace everybody in the loving arms of *their* conviction. But how few are willing to give up their convictions, throw them all in the middle of the pot, and just accept God. When that is proposed, human consciousness comes to the fore. No, that would wipe out the very thing we are trying to perpetuate.

If there is something within you that responds and agrees when I say to you that the kingdom of God is within you and must ultimately be experienced there, you have accepted the first simple bit of truth that has been known all through the ages and is just being repeated in the Infinite Way. When you feel the response within you that error is not something that has power, something that you have to fear or battle, but something you can well forget if you will turn your whole attention to having an actual experience of God within you, then you have agreed on the part of the teaching that concerns the nature of error. Once you have seen that realization, an experience of God within you, dispels anything that is in the nature of error, you have agreed with us on the teaching, and you see there is nothing deep about it: it is just acknowledging that error, in and of itself, could have no power. It is only in the absence of God that we have two powers at war with each other.

Real Prayer Has No Words

It is through prayer that we make contact with God. It is through prayer that we live and move and have our being in God. Prayer is the connecting link between our human identity and our spiritual identity. Prayer is that which dissolves our humanness into our divinity. That brings us to the question, "If prayer is the answer, what is prayer?"

Sometimes we have to teach the negative in order to arrive at the positive, and this is particularly true with prayer. Since most persons have some idea of what they think prayer is, there is no way to teach the nature of prayer until they get rid of all those ideas. The most important and shocking thing to remember is that real prayer does not exist in any church except when an individual goes there and sits in the silence. Real prayer has never been read from a platform, a desk, an altar, or voiced from any church platform.

Prayer has no words. We cannot pray in words or thoughts, and until we overcome the use of words and thoughts, we are not in prayer. That is simply stated, but the difficulty is to arrive at the ability to pray, which means to arrive at the ability to overcome the use of words and thoughts. Twenty-seven years in this work have convinced me that God cannot be reached through the human mind. Regardless of how noble our thoughts, we are far from reaching God. We cannot reach God with words.

Although the human mind itself cannot be used to gain entrance to God, God can use the human mind through which to reveal Itself to us. God can impart Itself to us in words and thoughts, but we cannot use words and thoughts to reach God. We cannot use our mind to reach God, but God can use our mind as an avenue of awareness to reach us. Our mind is an instrument through which we can open ourselves in a state of receptivity, and then God can flow in, with or without words or thoughts, and impart Itself to us. But we cannot use words or thoughts to reach God.

Prayer is opening ourselves to an inflow from God, Spirit, Soul, Consciousness. Actually, it is touching the depths of our own inner, unknown, infinite Being, and we are reaching back to let It spring up into our awareness and tell us things that we never knew before, in other words, to impart Itself, Its presence, and Its power to us.

Let nobody doubt that God is infinite, omnipotent, omnipresent, eternal, immortal, and indivisible. Because of this, where God is, there is nothing left of a destructive, injurious, or finite nature. Therefore, the only getting that we have to do is not to get a deep understanding or knowledge out of books. What we have to get is an awareness, a realization of that Presence. Where It is, error just is not. Discords evaporate into nothingness in the presence of this Spirit.

He that dwelleth in the secret place
of the most High shall abide
under the shadow of the Almighty.

A thousand shall fall at thy side,
and ten thousand at thy right hand;
but it shall not come nigh thee.

Psalm 91:1,7

Chapter Eight

God Realized

In meditation God reveals Itself to us and, in revealing Itself, It becomes the presence and power that takes over and governs our experience. If we think of going into meditation believing that it is going to overcome some problem or remove some obstacle, we defeat our purpose and prevent its activity. The reason we stress the nature of error is to remind ourselves that we are not seeking the realization of God for the purpose of overcoming error but, with an understanding that error has no power, we are turning within only for God-realization, and not for any purpose, that is, not to achieve anything. The only achievement is God-realization itself. To have a thought beyond that is to jeopardize our success.

We do not go to God to *get* something as if God were withholding it and as if our going would persuade Him to loosen up. We go to God only for the experience of communion, to sit in the presence of God, to feel the hand of God, and to be touched with the Spirit by the grace of God. That is enough, and when that happens, the discords of human experience begin to fade.

The Nature of Gratitude

It is right for us to enjoy spiritual grace translated into terms of human harmony and peace, but we cannot gain them by going to God solely for that purpose. Students will often feel a greater sense of gratitude for the healing of some so-called serious problem than they will for the healing of some minor thing. In our work that is rank error because it does not lie within our power to heal a headache or a cancer. But a realization of the presence of God reveals harmony where there was discord. Therefore, what we achieve for those who turn to us for help is the realization of God's presence, and whether it removes a headache or a cancer is incidental. It will do whatever is necessary, and sometimes far more than we could ever dream about. It is more far reaching than the immediate object we may have in mind.

To express gratitude in a different way for the healing of a headache than for the healing of a cancer is to misunderstand the whole object and purpose of this work, which is to bring God to us as a living reality, as a living presence. Then it is the function of God to dispel the whole of the illusory, limited, finite picture. To God it can make no difference whether it appears as a simple physical, mental, moral, or financial claim or as a very large or serious one. It would be impossible for God to meet a need for $100, but to be stumped by the need for $10,000.

The need, therefore, is not for a particular thing or condition. As the spiritual activity brings to light the realization of God, it will appear as harmony, whether the discord has appeared as a headache, a stomach ache, corns, bunions, calluses, or whether as a cancer, consumption, or polio. It makes no difference to the Spirit. When we understand that, we understand the nature of spiritual gratitude, because then gratitude has nothing to do with the degree of the demonstration.

To think of this work merely in the sense of healing some

particular physical, mental, moral, or financial problem is to limit it and to cheat ourselves of the opportunity of living in God's grace, for once we become aware of that grace operating in our experience, there is no end. There is no such thing as receiving a healing spiritually and having its effect stopped at any period of our human experience unless we choke it off, saying, "Ah, I've had the healing I was looking for. Isn't that grand!" Then, of course, we, ourselves, have set the limitation and we have drawn a curtain and kept God on the outside.

To perceive the nature of the Infinite Way message and know that our goal is not healing but to realize the Christ, then, from the minute that the Christ touches us, it will be, as Jesus described it, like the planting of a seed, and from then on there will be crop after crop, with no limit to its unfoldment, because the spiritual seed must multiply itself endlessly. It is not a matter of understanding: it is a matter of knowing the truth and knowing what our goal is.

We hear and read much about God: God's greatness, God's allness, and the infinite nature of God and what God does. Then we look out on the world and come to the conclusion that It does not do all we thought It would do. In that we will be right because it is not knowing about God that does the work: it is God *realized.* God goes right on being God while all the wars are taking place, all the people are being killed, all the children are dying, and all the other horrors of human life are taking place. Only one thing stops them: God realized. Wherever there is a realization of God, the disintegrating processes of human experience stop. Wherever there is a realization of God, the sins, the diseases, and the deaths stop. Wherever there is a realization of God, man is given his freedom, not only spiritual freedom, but a spiritual freedom which becomes evident as physical, mental, moral, and financial freedom.

If we are called upon for healing, let us not expect that it is going to take place except in proportion to our realization of God. If we do not have that realization, our patients are not going to receive the benefit of healing, except that in the normal course of events nature may take care of them, but as far as spiritual healing is concerned, it takes place at the moment of God-realization.

Importance of Maintaining God-Awareness

The day comes when, after we have been called to this work and have been the instrument for a thousand or two thousand healings, we are living in such a state of consciousness, of God-realization, that we will not have to sit down with every call that comes to get a specific answer because we are more or less living in that state of awareness all the time. We have to go back into meditation only when the claims come that are of such a deep and persistent nature that they do not yield readily to our attained state of consciousness, and we may have to sit down and spend hours and sometimes days and nights in meditation. "This kind goeth not out but by prayer and fasting."[1] Sometimes we may have to get back into a state of God-consciousness in which we lose any sense of earth in order to bring out some healings, and if that is necessary, it should be done.

Ordinarily speaking, those of us who are sufficiently busy in this activity eventually come to a state of realization which never permits us to come down to earth again. We, therefore, do not have to climb up to heaven. The only thing that we have to do is to be sure that on certain days, week-ends, or weeks we go away somewhere to live on cloud ninety-nine. As long as we do that we will find that we are living more or less constantly in the consciousness of God. We cannot neglect those periods of meditation or we will come back to earth again. There is no way to prevent the mesmerism of the world from dragging us back except periods—which are not only hours in length, but days and nights, sometimes week-ends, and sometimes whole weeks—in which to get away from everything and just live in the Word itself.

At that time of our life, we cannot again indulge the human life of excessive social activity. Then is when we come to the end of that period of life. There can be a very little of family activities left, because all those things tend to carry us down to the world's level, since we cannot carry our social friends and family up to this level of consciousness.

If we have a problem of our own or a problem for someone we are helping, we do not take the attitude of "Let God do it," or "God will take care of it." The responsibility is on our shoulders to attain God-realization for this specific purpose, and then we can say, "Now, God will take care of it. It's in God's hands," because now God is on the scene. God is never on the scene in the human picture until God is realized, and that is why we have witnessed that during a war whole regiments have been carried through battles without loss because of some God-realized chaplains at the front.

Surrendering Material States of Consciousness

Where the spirit of God is realized, there is freedom, and the disease or problem yields, if not at first, as quickly as the patient is able to yield some of those materialistic states of consciousness that are holding him in bondage.

Although we never can approach this work with judgment, criticism, or condemnation of patients, that does not stop us from apprehending that they are being held in bondage by some form of materialistic concept of life. We do not judge them for it; we do not criticize them; we do not condemn them, because we know that at the moment they are doing the very best they can do, the same as we are doing the best we can do at any given moment, without any claims to having attained perfection. But we do realize that that is what is holding back their progress and we continue to attain God-realization for them until they do yield their materialistic concepts or whatever erroneous state of consciousness is holding them in bondage. Once that yields, the physical, mental, moral, or financial condition also yields. The healing agency is the realization of the Christ. Any and every problem will yield in proportion to our faithfulness in attaining that Spirit.

From the "Good Old Days" to Spiritual Days

Out here we seem to have a world of physical form, not only with physical and material harmonies but also physical and material discords or inharmonies: sins, diseases, lacks. Let us acknowledge that the pendulum swings at times from periods of miserable materiality to other periods of good materiality, so that all of us have heard of, and some of us have experienced, what is called "the good old days."

There always have been periods of good old days and, strangely enough, in those very years which were our good old days, others were finding those days very tough ones. Then there are periods when we have had very hard times, and others were finding them the very good old days. Now there comes the possible transition from neither good material days nor bad material days to the experience of spiritual days, and spiritual days are always completely harmonious. It is that transition we are trying to bridge.

In the good old days, we solved our international problems with material force, by war. We overcame the sins of the world by incarcerating offenders in prisons, more force. If we attained peace through war, it never lasted. Always peace has been followed by war, and usually a more destructive one than the one before. There have been periods of great prosperity on earth, but they have been followed by periods of panic and depression, which came to be accepted as the normal cycle—periods of prosperity, then boom and bust.

There will be no change from that cycle until there is a change of base, and that change of base comes through spiritual realization. Years ago I maintained that no world peace would ever come through a human organization. It never has and it never will. Yet the day is close at hand when the United Nations will serve as an instrument that will maintain a greater sense of peace than before. But it will not be the United Nations doing it. It will be the United Nations being used by those spiritually minded individuals, those men of good will, who use that organization through which to channel their spiritual good will. That is now coming into expression.

Unless in our individual lives we can show forth harmony through the realized Christ, through a realization of God, we are not an example to our neighbors, our community, or to the world, and we can have no influence upon them. Preaching the Word will do little or nothing. What will help is sitting in our own homes and demonstrating it, drawing to us those who are ready for that experience and who in their turn go out into the world to perform whatever their function is to be.

Our Christ-Realization Touches the Lives of Those Who Are Receptive

Having acknowledged that there are physical, mental, moral, and financial discords in the world and having acknowledged that they can be brought to an end only by our individual Christ-realization, let our goal be to attain that realization. The kingdom of God is within us. We cannot reach God by thinking thoughts, although we can ponder passages of scripture until we settle down into peace and a state of receptivity. In the final analysis, the word of God has to come to us from within, from the depth of our being to our awareness, until we feel the Presence, the peace that passes all understanding. Thus established, we know that these things out here are only the "arm of flesh; but with us is the Lord our God to help us."[2] With that realization, what is left out there but "an arm of flesh," nothing to it, no presence, no power, whether germs, infection, contagion, evil men, evil plots, or plans? They all come to nothing in the presence of the realized Christ—not in the presence of a lot of human wisdom or knowledge—only in the presence of the realized Christ.

Furthermore, it would be an impossibility for me to sit here day in and day out, night in and night out, and have this conscious realization of the Christ and not have a group of people, near and far, come under the influence of that realized Christ and respond to It. But since God is no respecter of persons, it would also be an impossibility for you to sit in your home and actually achieve the realization of the Christ, feel that presence and power and not have it influence the lives of others. Sometimes, sad to relate, it may not affect the lives of those we would most like it to affect. Sadly enough, it may not affect the members of our family or friends we think need it most, because they have not yet the readiness for it.

The Master reveals that we have to forget our mother and father, our sister and brother, and our husband and wife. If they want to go to hell, we have to let them. But our life must be lived for the benefit of those, whether our own or not, who are seeking the kingdom of God. We have to open our heart, mind, and soul and give of our labors, whether to strangers or members of enemy countries makes no difference. If they are seeking the kingdom of God, our life is dedicated to them and our life is removed from those nearest and dearest to us by family ties if they will not bring themselves into our orbit. We dare not live for our own but for God's own. That is one of the prices we pay in this work. After a while many of our friends and relatives, if not most of them, and sometimes all of them, drift away from us, and we find our life is dedicated to "ye my disciples,"[3] rather than to our mother or brother, or sister or father.

We cannot have periods of meditation in which we are touched by the Spirit without blessing someone somewhere on earth, without touching the lives of individuals, sometimes in the highest places in the world. We may not know who they are. Whether they are high in politics, statesmanship, church circles, university circles, or civic life, we have no way of knowing, but eventually some of those whom we have touched may come to our knowledge. They are drawn to us out of all the world and eventually cross our path.

Our function is to attain more and more of this Christ-realization, for that is our particular contribution. First of all, it is our particular contribution to our own life. To live in constant and conscious God-realization is to live a joyous, satisfied, and satisfying life, for ourselves individually, but beyond that, it becomes our contribution to the world.

Our ultimate destiny is not a material but a spiritual destiny, and we can fulfill it only as we begin to fulfill our function in the place where we are now. There is nothing more spiritual about healing sick people than there is about keeping a set of books. Eventually, we see that just patching up people's bodies is not a very spiritual enterprise either. There is a higher mission for us. It is a spiritual mission, and it is attained only in proportion as we attain Christ-realization and find that we are waking somebody up out of his materiality and revealing a spiritual way of life to that person. Then we begin to see what the spiritual function is.

Aids to Attaining the Christ-Realized Mind

Our spiritual function is to be the light of the world so that those walking around in gross darkness can receive a measure of that light. That does not leave any room for a holier-than-thou-attitude. It does not leave any room for self-righteousness. We know all too well out of what we have come and how far we still are from the goal. Of all things the saddest part of this experience is that the more spiritual light we receive the unhappier we are, because the more nearly we become aware of what perfection is, the more we realize how far we are missing it. Whether or not we find it difficult to take, we have to go through the experience of knowing this.

Realization is demonstration. Realization is that spiritual impulse, that spirit of the Lord which establishes harmony, freedom, and peace, and there is no other way. Studying books or hearing tapes is the path that leads to the goal. It is like priming the pump. On occasion I do it myself. I pick up a book and read a paragraph or a page, sometimes eight or ten pages, and all of a sudden something registers with me. Then I put the book down, and I can sit there and go on in to my meditation.

Ever since 1947, I have been trying to teach meditation and here and there I have succeeded. We have students in every part of the globe who have attained the ability to meditate with sufficient depth to attain Christ-realization. Both *Practicing the Presence*[4] and *The Art of Meditation*[5] provide the actual practice and atmosphere to help students find easier steps toward meditation. These books are good to use as a basis because they seem to provide a foundation that enables students to grasp the principles of the Infinite Way. Infinite Way writings provide constant reminders that the nature of God, the nature of error, and the nature of prayer are prerequisites for deeper realization so that anyone who is serious enough can achieve God-realization and the actual experience of the Christ.

The first stage of our reading is, of course, to clear out all the nonsense about religious beliefs that we have picked up in a lifetime, and then the second thing, when we have fairly well cleared out such beliefs, is to gain the realization that what we are after is an understanding of the nature of God and the nature of prayer, and from there on our goal is the realization of it.

Have I made it clear that we do not change evil to good, sickness to health, or lack to abundance? The goal is attaining Christ-realization, which in its turn dissolves the so-called material picture and renders all the armies of the aliens the "arm of flesh," making of them nothing.

All of this has to do with you and with me as individuals. "Ye shall know the truth, and the truth shall make you free."[6] A mind in ignorance of truth cannot make anyone free. A mind in ignorance of truth is in bondage. The next step then is to have a mind imbued with truth. As human beings we have a mind filled with spiritual ignorance, and it has no healing or liberating power. If the mind is imbued with ignorance, it is full of superstition and fear. There is no healing in that mind. The mind imbued with truth has lost its ignorance, its superstition, its fear, and so the mind imbued with truth becomes the Christ realized mind.

We have nothing to do with what God is or with what God does at this minute. We have to do with us. To what degree do we have a mind imbued with ignorance, superstition, and fear? To what extent do we have a mind imbued with spiritual truth, that is, with the awareness of only one power instead of two? To what degree is our mind imbued with a confidence that Pilate can have no power over us? To what degree is our mind imbued with the truth that germs, infection, or contagion are just the "arm of flesh," nothingness? To what degree is our mind imbued with the truth that no person, no circumstance, or no condition except the realized Christ has power?

When we understand this, the way of our spiritual development becomes simple, because now we are dealing with just you and me. We cannot look around and wonder about anybody else's demonstration. Our only concern is our own, nor can we cry out against God because God has nothing to do with our degree of ignorance or enlightenment. That has to do with whether or not we are devoting ourselves to attaining enlightenment.

It is identically the same principle when our practitioners look at a condition of sin, disease, death, or limitation. There is only one thing with which they must concern themselves: what degree of truth is their mind imbued with at that moment, because on that depends the degree of the demonstration. It is not a question of whether there is some God to take pity on us, or whether God is going to reward us because we have lived a good life. God isn't. God has a way of hammering away at human good and human evil. He takes His toll of both the good and the evil, making no distinction between the good and the evil. There is only one distinction made and that is the degree of spiritual enlightenment.

Mind Imbued with Truth Opens Consciousness

When we are facing a problem of our own or of another and can bring to our conscious remembrance all we know of spiritual truth, we will then have a mind imbued with truth, and we will be able to bring the presence and power of truth to bear on that problem. Then, when we have thought and voiced all the truth that is within range of our immediate awareness, we sit and let the Father in and that completes the demonstration. The healing work is not accomplished by remembrances of truth alone. "Man shall not live by bread alone,"[7] by knowledge. The word of God itself, the very presence of God, must come into our consciousness.

There are two stages in our spiritual development, two stages in our meditation, and two stages in our healing work. In each case, they are the same two. What is truth, not what is the truth about this error? What is truth? And the truth is that "where the Spirit of the Lord is, there is liberty."[8] Where truth is, there is no error. Where life is, there is no death. The kingdom of God is within us. The kingdom of God is wherever it is realized. The kingdom of God is a "peace be still"[9] to any form of error.

Wherever Jesus walked, the presence of God walked with him because he lived and dwelt continuously in the realization of God. Wherever he walked, he was a benediction, a blessing,

Even to touch the hem of his robe brought forth a healing because he lived in God, and God lived in him. Wherever he went the discords fled. But have we ever read of his wanting or trying to demonstrate anything for himself? Even when he was anhungered, he refused to demonstrate food. His attitude was: "It is God's function to feed me. I'll wait until God sets a table before me. I will not work miracles, even though I have nowhere to lay my head." But every night he slept some place, and he was an invited guest for luncheons, dinners, and whatever meals he needed.

Being Receptive to the Spirit of God

When the spirit of God is upon us, It provides, not only for us but for all those who are within range of our consciousness. If we dwell in the word of God and let the word of God dwell in us, we are filled with the spirit of God. When the spirit of the Lord God is upon us, we are anointed to heal the sick, comfort those that mourn, and restore the lost years of the locust—but only when the spirit of the Lord is upon us. The presence of God is a law of annihilation to all discord. Wherever Jesus walked that spirit of God in him proved to be an annihilation to error of any and every form.

Eventually each one is transformed by the renewing of the mind. Let us not forget that a mind imbued with ignorance is not going anywhere spiritually, but a mind imbued with truth is going to bring about healing and supplying. The mind that is imbued with truth forms its own conditions, just as a mind imbued with ignorance forms its conditions. The mind imbued with truth becomes the body beautiful—whether it is a physical, financial, or moral form.

So when the spirit of God is upon us, the errors of this world have no power. They become the "arm of flesh." We need not fight. Instead, let us get the spirit of the Lord and let the spirit of the Lord dwell in us. Then the enemies fight among themselves and destroy each other.

I shall not fear what mortal man or mortal conditions
can do unto me.
The spirit of the Lord God Almighty
is my answer.
In Thy presence is life evermore,
life everlasting. Thy grace is my sufficiency
in all things. I need not seek health
or supply for myself or another.
I need not seek peace for myself or another,
safety or security. I seek only Thy grace,
which is my sufficiency.
"Where the Spirit of the Lord is, there is liberty."

And all these things have I remembered,
Father, and all these things do I know.
Yet there is one thing more.
Let Thy word be spoken unto me.
Let Thy mantle fall on my shoulders.
Let Thy spirit fill me.
Bless all those on whom my thought rests.
Friend or foe, saint or sinner,
Father, forgive them "seventy times seven"
for they know not what they do.
Let Thy spirit be upon all men.

By now thought has quieted down so that there are longer periods of listening and shorter intervals of voicing or thinking something.

It may be we have to be patient until it comes but, in one of those intervals of peace and quiet, that deep breath or that inner assurance comes of the Presence, and then the work is done. Whether it is for ourselves or for another, our part of it is finished. The Spirit is on the field, and It is dissolving whatever of material sense needs dissolving. It can be an instantaneous healing or it can be a slow one, depending on whether or not the patient or student is really ready to relinquish some of the material things and thoughts that have cluttered up life. But the result is inevitable.

Tape Recorded Excerpts
Prepared by the Editor

A cardinal principle of the Infinite Way is that it must never be organized but is to remain forever a movement in consciousness. The excerpt below is an example of Joel's undeviating stand on this principle which is unique to the Infinite Way.

"Organization and the Infinite Way"

"As you know, the one thing that I pray ardently for is that this work will never be organized as a religion. One day the thought came to me, 'You are taking a lot of work on your shoulders and doing a lot of hard work, all to prevent organization.' All this work that I do could be done by others with just the tiniest bit of an organization, and to avoid that I do a lot of work personally that could be done by others. The thought came to me one day, 'I wonder if that isn't all fruitless if five or ten years after I retire from the scene, somebody won't come along and slap a beautiful corporation together or, as someone wrote me, 'I have a wonderful idea for an unorganized organization.'

"'The Voice came to me directly and said, 'Be not concerned; the source of this work will never permit it to be organized, and whoever tries will be removed.' That's what the Master meant when he said, 'My words will not pass away.' He knew the source of the Word. If God is the source of the Infinite Way, be assured of this: The Infinite Way will never be organized because that must not be God's purpose. And who is to thwart God's purpose?"

Joel S. Goldsmith. "Atmosphere of Prayer and Higher Concept of Prayer," *The 1953 Los Angeles Practitioner Class. Tape 5:2.*

Chapter Nine

Starting the Mystical Life

The glorification of a human being is never the goal of a spiritual study. Rather is it the annihilation of the human being. When Paul teaches that we need to "die daily,"[1] he is not playing with language. He is very serious about that. So, too, when the Master states, "For whosoever will save his life shall lose it: and whosoever will lose his life for my sake shall find it,"[2] he is stating a spiritual principle.

Many metaphysical teachings would have us believe that by demonstrating health and supply we are doing the will of God. In the very earliest days of metaphysical healing, there was no such intent. Healing was only a means of proving that the principle was true, but the principle was the important thing and not the healing. What followed and still continues could happen in our work. Those in the Infinite Way who carry on a healing ministry or conduct tape meetings usually give some instruction to those who come to them, explaining the principles that students do not understand, the how and the why of them, and helping them with healing work. What inevitably happens is that if those who are conducting the work are at all consecrated they soon become so busy with healing work that there is no time left for teaching, instruction, or imparting the message. So there again begins the same old round of sitting in an office and acting as an aspirin tablet or a foot plaster to those who bring their bodies to the office. That really should not happen in our work.

The metaphysics of the Infinite Way is made up of the letter of truth and, while studying that, it is natural that our health, our living conditions, our business, and our human relationships all improve. But these are not our goal. Our goal is to achieve a consciousness of the mysticism of the Infinite Way, that is, that part of the teaching which brings us into conscious union with God. If the attainment of material things were our goal, we could very quickly have a million followers. But that is not our goal. Our goal is the revelation of principles known to the mystics of all ages, found in the literature of all peoples, but principles which have been lived only by the few.

Two Bible Statements, the Foundation of the Infinite Way

A child can more readily accept spiritual teaching and spiritual living than can an adult. The reason is that spiritual living is such a simple way of life, so simple that we, as grownups, find it difficult. There is no one truth to which we are limited, and yet if there were no other statements of truth available, any real statement of truth is sufficient to carry an individual into heaven.

My whole life work probably came out of two Bible passages. Although I know, use, and understand many others, it would make no difference to me if they all were wiped out, or made illegal, as long as I would be permitted to keep just these two. "Cease ye from man, whose breath is in his nostrils: for wherein is he to be accounted of?"[3] and "My kingdom is not of this world."[4] Those two are enough for me and have been enough on which to found the entire Infinite Way work and carry it around the globe. If there were no others, those two would suffice.

The Word of God Is the Substance of All Form

There is also another one that has played an important part in my experience, because I have witnessed its miracles with some of our students. It is so simple, and so well know to you, that you will hardly believe its importance. "Man shall not live by bread alone, but by every word that proceedeth out of the mouth of God."[5] If I could not have the first two statements, I would take that one. There is enough bread, meat, wine, water, life, and resurrection in that one statement to carry anybody into heaven. "Man shall not live by bread alone"—by form, by that which is in expression, by that which is effect, "but by every word that proceedeth out of the mouth of God."

When temptations have come to me in the form of needing or requiring something, it was necessary only to return to that one statement and realize that man shall not live by *anything* that is in this world. He shall not live by anything that exists as effect: man shall live by every word that proceeds out of Consciousness, out of the mouth of God.

This does not mean that we live by the words in the Bible or in metaphysical statements, for they are form and forms are effect: creatures, not creators. It means literally that we shall live by every word we receive within ourselves, within our consciousness, every word that can come out of the Infinite Invisible into form as our conscious awareness. That immediately takes us back to receptivity, to meditation, to listening for the "still small voice,"[6] to becoming consciously aware of the presence of God.

It would be an utter impossibility to receive the word of God and to find something lacking in our experience, for the word of God is the substance of all form and, therefore, takes the form of whatever it is that is necessary for our experience at any given moment. It would make no difference if our need were for another book of truth, another teaching of truth, another teacher of truth, or for dollar bills. As long as our thought was not on the need but on attaining that inner impartation of the Word, the fulfillment would take place in any and every form.

Speak Only from the Spirit

Our study is primarily to enable us to achieve a state of consciousness in which or through which we can receive that Word. That is the reason so much attention is given to the subject of meditation, not meditation from the standpoint of sitting for hours, waiting for the mind to become numb, but waiting minutes with a sense of inner expectancy for an impartation from within. This state of consciousness is developed, not minute by minute, not hour by hour, but second by second. Only those who practice to the extent that they would not think of crossing a doorsill—going in or going out—without waiting for that one second, just to prepare thought for the inflow; only those who never eat or drink without that momentary pause for the Word, before even the food is taken in, only those who never undertake even marketing, buying, selling, moving, or traveling without that pause that really refreshes will receive the Word that comes into consciousness and renews. That pause gives a whole fresh inner life, inner vigor, a renewed activity of soul, of mind, and of body. Never undertake anything, not even your day's housework or your day's business without that pause that gives God the opportunity to come into expression.

When writing or speaking to a patient, speak only from the Spirit. Your verbal words are worthless unless spoken in and from the Spirit. Anything you would say to a patient or student would constitute the cold letter of truth which kills. Statements such as, "Oh, you know you are spiritual"; or "You know this isn't real"; or "Oh, you know there is no pain"; or "You know God will take care of it"; are misleading and usually prove to be untrue because they are spoken from the mind, and they are spoken from memory. They are not spoken out of inspiration. No one can utter truth except when in the Spirit. Only when you are in that consciousness that permits the Spirit to come through, can you for a single moment believe that what you say is the word of God that is quick and sharp and powerful, and goes right to the root of the matter.

Be Open to the Spirit Within

Every activity of our human experience is divine, even in the merchandise mart, if it is permeated by the activity of the Spirit within us. There are not, rightly speaking, two worlds: a spiritual one and a material one. There are two worlds, in effect, at the present time, in this world, certainly. There is a spiritual universe and there is the material world, which rapidly is disintegrating by destroying itself. Rightly understood however, every human experience is a divine one, *if* it is imbued with the Spirit, *if* the word of God has come into consciousness to perform it. "For he performeth the thing that is appointed for me."[7] "The Lord will perfect that which concerneth me."[8] In the experience of the world, it is not true.

It is not God that is going up and down this world doing the horrible things we see. It is the absence of God doing it. It is only when individuals open themselves and permit themselves to become permeated with the Word that they can say, "Everything that I perform is really God performing it in action. I am but the instrument, the outlet, through which God flows." We have no right to claim that, except in proportion as every move of our day and night is preceded by that momentary pause that permits the inflow of God.

In answering the telephone, practice lifting up the receiver and pausing for a moment to let the Christ in before saying, "Hello, who's there?" It is surprising what miracles takes place on the telephone when that pause comes in before the first words are spoken. Then there are not two human beings coming together, each with their individual identities, individualities, interests, problems, and profits, but the Christ comes in as a cement between these two individual states of consciousness, intent on one purpose. It is only necessary that *one* perform this ritual of the pause for the simple reason that one with God is a majority. Where the Spirit enters, It will quickly annihilate or remove from experience that which is uncongenial to It.

Too few of our students take advantage of that opportunity for a pause before any and every activity of the day. If I, of myself, am performing whatever work there is to be done, a sense of limitation comes in. My memory may be at fault, my skill inadequate to the job, or my experience lacking. But if I make room for the Spirit to enter, then any lack of experience, education, memory, or anything else necessary will be disposed of and, in some way, God will be the leaven unto that experience, and harmony will prevail. No one has of himself sufficient wisdom; no one has sufficient strength or power; no one has sufficient intelligence. But God is infinite, and *His* understanding is infinite. His strength shall be my strength; His power, my power; His joy, my joy. Without that, life becomes meaningless.

The Mystical Aspect of the Infinite Way

"Man shall not live by bread alone." Take that word "bread" and think of it as meaning that man shall not live by his own understanding, his own experience, his own education, his own beliefs, convictions, or concepts. Man shall not live by his money, his investments, his business, or his capacity. Man shall not live by anything that has effect. Man shall not even live by the truth that he has learned out of books, but man shall live "by every word that proceedeth out of the mouth of God."

A dozen times a day the ear will be open, and into it will come guidance, direction, wisdom, and the experience of love, peace, joy, and dominion. You know that experiences are coming into your life which you, as a person, were never responsible for, things exceeding your own dreams.

This is the meaning of the mystical side of the Infinite Way. It means to live no longer by the economy of the world, no longer by the traditions of the world, but always by an inner grace. Miracles have been wrought by the passage, "My grace is sufficient for thee."[9] Just think of replacing the "I need money for this, that, or some other thing" with "My grace is sufficient for thee" in all things, and let that grace take form in whatever way It will. The only difficulty is that we are very apt to believe that we know what form that grace should take, and we keep watching for it. In watching for it, we miss it when it comes, because usually it does not come in the expected form. God, in His infinite wisdom and love, bestows on us not those things that we believe we need, but those things which are spiritual life, water, and wine to our experience.

To Realize "I Have" Is to Rise Above Limitation

Another passage that can bring great spiritual fruitage is: "I have meat to eat that ye know not of."[10] How many meanings that word "meat" has! Amazing things happen with the first two words, "I have." We demonstrate whatever there is in our consciousness. If we have *I have not* in our consciousness, we demonstrate *have not.* Multiplication is a law, and if you plant the seed of *have not,* you will be surprised how it can multiply. It really can and does, and the *have nots,* the Bible says, we always have with us. The seed you plant is the crop you grow, and to abide in the consciousness of "I have not," "I need," "I require," "I desire" is to keep right on multiplying *have not.* No fulfillment can come, because no seeds of fulfillment have been planted.

The seeds of fulfillment are *I have:* "I have meat to eat that ye know not of." What does that meat consist of? The word of

God, that word which we hear in the ear: "I have divine substance. I have the presence of God; I have the mind of God, that mind which was in Christ Jesus."

Is there more than one life? As we look out into the garden and watch our coconuts, bananas, and all the various flowers there, asking if each one has a life of its own, we quickly perceive that it is the same ground, the same fertilizer, the same rain, and the same sunshine, and we come to the conclusion there must be only one life out there.

So, the *meat* I have is the awareness that I have but one life, and that is God's life, not mine. My life is not my life; God's life constitutes my life. There is no place where God's life leaves off and mine begins any more than there is a place where electricity stops and the electricity of the light bulb begins. There is just one electricity; there is just one spiritual life. There is no place where the sun stops and the sunbeam begins. The sunbeam is the sun itself, appearing to us in an individual way. If you go high enough in the clouds, you will see there are no sunbeams: there is just the sun shining.

There is no such thing as your life or mine; therefore, there is no such thing as a young life, an old life, a strong life or a weak life, a well life or a sick life: there is only one life. That is the *meat* I have that the world does not know, the truth that God is my life without beginning and without end. It is that which makes it possible for the mystic to know the past, the present, and the future, not in any fortune-telling sense, but in an actual awareness of the spiritual realities as they are, and as they always will be, and through that, the ability to predict what is going to happen in the human world. That is not based on clairvoyant powers.

If, for example, you saw somebody sticking his hand into a fire, it would not be difficult for you to predict that he would get burned. If you saw somebody imbibing a quart of whiskey every day, it would not take much ability to predict that he would end up as an alcoholic. Every time you witness a violation of law, you can usually predict what the penalty is going to be. You only have to see a person steal a few times to know that he will end up in jail. It is an inevitability. You become a prophet on that score; you know the end from seeing the beginning. So it has been with many persons who have predicted the future. They knew it by watching people violating spiritual law, and they knew the inevitability of the consequences, whether for an individual, a nation, or a group of nations.

I have meat, wine, water, bread, resurrection, life eternal, not because of myself and not because of my study. I have them as the grace of God. Everyone has them, but no one benefits from them except in proportion to a conscious realization of this truth. Therein lies one of the mysteries that the religious world apparently has not discovered. They teach God's presence and power in the world and the almightiness of God. But they have not taught that all of that is of no avail except in proportion to a person's conscious realization of it, thereby bringing himself into at-one-ment with it. People have been taught that there is a God, and because of that, ultimately all is going to be well. No, that is not true. There is a God, and all is ultimately going to be well to those who fulfill the terms, and the terms are, "Ye shall know the truth, and the truth shall make you free,"[11] *Ye* shall know truth. It has nothing to do with your neighbor. "A thousand shall fall at thy side, and ten thousand at thy right hand; but it shall not come nigh"[12] you who consciously know the truth and dwell in it and *let it dwell in you.*

How Spiritual Truths Come Alive

Before you can let the truth dwell in you, you must know what the truth is. The truth can be found in its fullness in the Gospels. There is no need to add to the truth that is there, plus the explanation found in St. Paul's writings. The only function of work like the Infinite Way is to bring these ancient teachings to light again, to make them live in human consciousness, and to teach the value of learning them, abiding in them, and living them. But a teaching such as the Infinite Way has never added anything to what is to be found in the New Testament. It is merely taking one passage like "I have meat," "My grace is sufficient for thee," or any passage, and making it come alive instead of just reading it and believing that because it is in the Bible, or even because of our much repetition of it, it will do anything for us.

The Master warned against vain repetitions. Do not think that by repeating these statements of truth they will go to work for you. These statements must be lived, one at a time. Infinite Way writings are but exemplifications or enlargements of the specific truths of scripture, some from the old Hebrew masters, some from those who had attained their Christhood, some from the more modern Hebrew masters, some from those who later because Christian mystics, and some Oriental mystics who went before. They are all the same truth merely voiced in the language of a particular nation, and a particular era.

God speaks to men as much today as at any time in the history of the world. There is no lack of God speaking. The only lack is in man's hearing, and that is because we have lost the knack of momentarily waiting for the spirit of God to enter our consciousness and take over.

We are at the period of development in the message of the Infinite Way where it is assumed that our students know the letter of truth, that is, that they know that there is only one power, and have developed themselves to the place where they no longer fear negative powers. It is assumed they have attained some measure of the consciousness that "Thou couldest have no power at all against me, except it were given thee from above,"[13] and that all that constitutes the metaphysics of this message has been learned, so that at no time will there be a danger of falling away from the correct letter and thereby endangering their spiritual progress. With that correct letter of truth understood and intellectually digested, there comes that part of the experience when our major effort must be placed on that pause, on understanding how to attain spiritual grace.

Our life is lived by spiritual grace, not by might, not by power, not by physical might and not by mental powers, but by a spiritual grace. It is the gift of God. Everything that concerns our life is a gift of God. It is not attained by the physical strivings, the physical labors, or the mental powers that are developed, but by their opposite, by the ability to be filled with the Spirit, that the grace of God may take over and find expression. That is the goal of our life. That is our attainment. But, can you not see that as long as our attention is focused on bettering human conditions or on attaining improved humanhood, we can in no way enter the spiritual kingdom?

At this stage it is virtually a "dying daily" to our human hopes and to our human ambitions. It is literally a giving up of the desire for those things that the world is destroying itself trying to get. At first that appears to be so transcendental that it is not only beyond our reach but even beyond what we desire. Actually, the effect of this transcendental awareness fulfills us in our human experience. It seems to add more of those things that the world wants and cannot get. It is very much like the discovery that many of you have made that whatever it is you want, make up your mind you would not have it as a gift, and watch how quickly it starts chasing you about. It won't give you any rest until it sits on your shoulders, but you must not want it. You must be indifferent to it.

That goes even for life itself, or what we call the human expression of life. Many and many a sick person has regained health only when he has reached the point of saying, "Well, Father, You can have my physical life if You want it, or if the devil wants is more than You do, let the devil have it. My concern is not for my physical life but for my spiritual life." It is surprising how quickly they find out that not only their spiritual life but their physical one comes back too.

There is no sacrifice, nor is there any ascetism in the truly spiritual life. It is only that in opening ourselves to the grace of the Spirit many of the thing that we thought of as worthwhile in our human life become meaningless and worthless. Now we would not have them as a gift and we wonder why we ever found them desirable and how it is that we missed the great spiritual forms of life that others knew about, but we never dreamed of.

I, *the Holy Word*

The word *I* is the only thing that is closer to you than breathing and nearer than hands and feet. The word *I* is the secret word which you must ponder within yourself. First of all, you must be careful not to go out and preach It or tell It to those who are still seeking loaves and fishes, because you would be putting a weapon in their hands—a two-edged sword that could turn and rend them. Many have been wrecked by the wrong understanding of the words *I Am.* They have believed that It applied to their humanhood, and they have erroneously tried to make their human selves God; or they have tried to make *I* play God to their human wants and wishes and desires, and in that they have come upon sad days.

Sacredly and secretly, take the word *I* into your consciousness; pick up the Gospels, read them through, and note particularly that "I will never leave thee, nor forsake thee,"[14] that "I am the bread of life,"[15] so that when you say, "I have meat the world knows not of," bread or wine or water, you know what that bread, meat, or wine is. It is *I*. *I* have meat. Wherever that *I* is, there is meat. Not only do I *have* meat: *I am* the meat, *I am* the bread, not only do I *have* bread: *I* Itself *is* the bread. Only as you hear that word *I* in gentleness and in sacredness, do you come into God's actual presence within yourself.

I is the secret word. *I* is the holy word. *I* is the word that the Hebrews were never allowed to speak. They could think of God in any other terms; they could speak or write of God in any other terms, but only the priests, only those of the Holy Spirit and of holy awareness, were allowed to say the word *I.*

So it should be with us. In our human way we speak of "I, Joel," "I, Bill," or "I, Mary," but within ourselves we must learn to think of God as *I.* When we do, we say, "Oh, *that* is why the place whereon I stand is holy ground. It is because *I* is there." *I* is right where Joel is, and that is why where Joel is is holy ground, because *I* is there, and right where *I* is, even if it were in the desert, *I* would lead Joel to an oasis. It makes no difference if it takes three days, three weeks, or three years, it will come to those who abide patiently at the center of their being in the realization that the allness of life is already within them: they *have.*

I have, and I am. All that the Father has is mine.
All that God is, I am by virtue of I,
not by virtue of Joel.
That is the man who must die in order
that I may be reborn.
If you destroy this temple,
Jesus will not rebuild it.
Jesus could be dead in a tomb,
but I will rebuild it,
and Jesus will then walk the earth again.

I is the secret. *I* is that word which, when it is understood in its gentleness and in its sacredness, becomes outwardly our supply, our companionship, our success, our joy, our inspiration. It is only then that humility can be properly understood. Humility comes only in proportion as we understand that God planted in us an inner grace, that which is to be with us unto the end of the world and our demonstration unto the end of the world. It is to go before us to "make the crooked places straight."[16] It is to go before us to prepare mansions for us. It is to be all things unto us. "I am the way, the truth, and the life,"[17] that *I,* the realization of that *I*—not looking outside to a God, not looking inside to a God, not looking up or down to a God to do something, just realizing *I* already is all. *I* already is about the Father's business.

You do not have to take thought for your life, what to eat, what to drink, or with what to be clothed, for that which is the *I* at the center of your being knows that you have need of these things, and it is Its good pleasure to give you the kingdom. But to interpose a desire, a need, or a requirement is to interfere with Its activity.

There is one erroneous premise that from the beginning has kept mankind from enjoying the presence and power of this *I* that is always with us, and that, we are told, is our knowledge of good and evil. It is that which prevents the *I* from functioning. We have decided what is good and what is evil. We have decided or been taught *who* is good and *who* is evil, what constitutes good and what constitutes evil, so that we have lived by bread alone, by our concepts of life, instead of by Life. We have even developed concepts of God and then have prayed to our concepts.

Accept I *in the Midst of You*

Hebrews have one concept of God; Protestants have other concepts of God; Catholics have a different one; the Mohammedans still a different one. All are praying, not to God, but to their particular concept of God, not realizing that this is idolatry. Is there any other God but *I?* I know not any. Can anyone define *I?* Can anyone analyze *I?* Can anyone describe *I?* No, indeed. There is no use trying to understand what *I* is, because when Joel says "I," and when you say "I," it is the same *I,* and yet you would never know that to look at us because of the different concepts we have of that *I.*

Do not try to understand what *I* is. Accept the truth that *I* is in the midst of you and that *I* goes before you, that *I* will never leave you. That *I* Itself is the bread, the wine, and the water. *I* is the resurrection. "Destroy this temple, and in three days I will raise it up."[18] In the wilderness, *I* will set a table before you. That was proved to Elijah when on one occasion the widow fed him—the poor widow. On other occasions, ravens fed him, or cakes were being baked on the stones when he awakened. Even when Joel sleeps, *I* it is that feeds him, whether It has to bring it through ravens, poor widows, rich widows, or businessmen. It makes no difference. *I* will always provide a way to reach the human need in fulfillment.

Only do not have needs: have *I*. Remember, "I have . . . a little oil in a cruse."[19] "We have here but five loaves, and two fishes."[20] *I* have bread, wine, water. "I am the resurrection, and the life."[21] Abide in that, and then, so that it does not become merely lip service, take those periods—at least twelve, twenty, thirty of them in a day on every occasion—just to listen, and then walk on about your business. Open that ear to the inflow. Nothing may outwardly take place at the moment, but every rightful thing will take place in its own way as the day proceeds.

We can bring this to the world only if we, as individual students, attain it. As we live a life of grace and our human lives attest to the presence and power of God, in that degree will others seek it of us. They will not seek it by our preaching it; they will not seek it by our teaching it: they will seek it only by our living it, demonstrating it, and then they will come and ask for it.

Chapter Ten

Surrendering the Human Sense of Health, Supply, and Peace

Although those of us on the spiritual path are to some extent the same persons we were when we first came to the study of spiritual wisdom, in some ways we have changed. We are now in a state of consciousness where we do not enjoy the same things we did before, nor are we understood by some members of our family and friends. As time goes on, this breach may widen until some members of our family become totally separated from us, and most of our friends will have gone their way. When that time comes, we either have no friends or we have made new friends on the spiritual path.

When we are trying to live out from spiritual consciousness, we no longer see eye to eye with those deeply engrossed in material consciousness. They cannot understand us, and we cannot understand them. For example, at the first sign of a sniffle, some member of our family may say, "Oh, have you taken an aspirin?" Immediately, our inner response would be, "Now, what power would that have?" We forget that perhaps only a few months ago such appearances would have been all-power and fear might have arisen. Now we think, "I know those things are effect. How can one effect touch another effect? I have access to the source." How ridiculous that must sound to those who still believe that God is all wrapped up in an aspirin tablet! In the same way, many of the things of this world that formerly troubled us, no longer bother us. Many of the things which we feared, we no longer fear. Many of the things which we enjoyed, we no longer enjoy.

Discord, Not God-Created

We came to a metaphysical teaching of one school or another with a specific problem, and we learned a very strange thing. We learned that we had to deny that we had it. In other words, here we were very sick and in pain, and we were told, "Oh, but you must deny that. You do not have it." It seemed ridiculous at first, but after a while we came to understand what our friends meant.

What the metaphysicians meant was that the sin, disease, false desire, inharmony, or discord was not a reality insofar as God was concerned, that is, that God had not created it; therefore, it had no permanent life or being. In that sense it was unreal. They really did not mean that it was unreal as far as your or my experience of the moment was concerned, although it certainly sounded that way. But even when we went around affirming and denying, it must have seemed to us somewhat ridiculous to say, "This isn't true, and I haven't got it, and it isn't real," when all the time it continued to pester us.

Some of us did finally realize what our metaphysical friends were telling us. This condition, whatever its name or nature, has no existence in or of God; it is not a reality with a law to sustain it. There is a law that sustains two times two is four. Nobody can break that. But if we come under the belief that two times two is five, someone can still tell us it is not real, that it has no law to sustain it, and that we cannot be made to suffer from it. But we are suffering from it. We are giving out five for every four, and this continues until we awaken and realize that five is really not the truth in relation to two times two. It is a belief which we overcome by knowing the mathematical principle.

So in our metaphysical work, regardless of the nature of our problem, it exists as far as we are concerned and we suffer from it. But it exists only because we have accepted the world-belief on that point much in the same way that at one time it was believed that a person could not go more than a few miles from shore because he would tumble off into space at the horizon. Those who accepted that had to stay close to shore, but there really was no such law, and one could have gone as far as he wanted to travel or as far as a boat could carry him. It took until 1492, however, for that to be demonstrated to the satisfaction of the world. Then what became of the limitation that held those who believed in such limitation to the shore? It disappeared. It was no longer accepted; it was no longer in their mind, and therefore it no longer manifested.

Real Gratitude

Within a few years those who come to a metaphysical teaching lose eighty to ninety percent of their ills and problems, because those ills and problems, which are so real to human sense by virtue of their having been accepted as reality by them, are now found to be non-reality, having no law to sustain them, no cause, and no foundation. We have learned how to eliminate them from our experience. We become ill and immediately say, "No, I can't be ill. This isn't reality. It has no law to sustain it. It has no cause in God and, whatever its physical or mental cause, it has no divine source, and therefore must instantly disappear." We soon learn how effective that is and how quickly our sickness disappears and health appears. After that, we live for many years, no longer in a physical sense of life, but more in a mental sense of life, and one in which discords disappear and harmonies appear.

During this period we develop a very strange complex. We get to the point where we say, "Oh, I'm not trying to change sickness into health or lack into abundance. I am trying to realize spiritual reality." We all come to that point, but, as a matter of fact at that stage, none of us means it. We are merely using words like that in order to overcome the discord so we can feel well and be happy that we have overcome some discord and then boast about how sick we were and how well we are now. But while it lasted, we said, "Oh, I'm not doing it to get well. I'm doing it to realize my Christhood."

It is a point of self-deception, and strangely enough, for a while it works. We really convince ourselves that we just want to realize our spiritual sense; we don't want to get well; we don't want to meet Saturday's rent; we don't want better business. But if that fever does not go down or the lump does not disappear, how worried we get, and when the fever *does* go or the rent *is* met, how quick we are to express gratitude!

From this point on we are not going to make much progress unless we perceive the nature of real gratitude and understand the real value of this type of work and life, which is far different from merely appreciating a physical healing. We are very grateful, not only in words, but in our expression of that gratitude financially. We are at that point where we express our gratitude in very liberal payments to a practitioner for every harmonious experience we enjoy through metaphysical or spiritual truth.

Now we have to take another step forward in gratitude to the point where we no longer express gratitude merely for the benefit that has come to us. Instead of being grateful for healings, for increased supply, or for any form of good that comes into our experience, we learn *why* we should be grateful, for *what* we should be grateful, and then inwardly we learn *how* to be grateful and express that gratitude tangibly.

The Meaning of Spiritual Integrity

In a spiritual teaching that takes us beyond metaphysics, we are at the point where we must have more spiritual integrity. When we say, "I'm not trying to get well," we have to mean it.

When we mouth some words such as, "I'm not looking for increased supply," we have to mean them. At this point of our unfoldment, our attitude must be, "Sick or well, rich or poor, what I am seeking is the Christ-experience. I am determined to have that if I have to have it with patches on my clothes, with a half empty stomach, or if I have to have it in pain or in health. The object of my life is spiritual awareness. If I get well in the process, good. If I don't it still will not matter because I have but one object, and it is not merely getting well, not merely having an abundance of supply, not merely being able to keep up with the Joneses. Now, I have a spiritual mission, which is as important to me as it was to the disciples when the Master said, 'Follow me, and I will make you fishers of men'.[1]" It was as if he were urging them to stop relying on their fishing for their supply.

That is not an easy state of consciousness to attain, not one we come to in one second, unless it is given to us by a divine inner grace. But it is one to which we must accustom ourselves, because eventually we have to reach it. Sooner or later, the lesson will be brought home to us that just exchanging sickness for health is not a very spiritual demonstration. Exchanging some monetary lack for monetary abundance is not necessarily a great spiritual demonstration. Even if we achieve health and wealth, we will not have achieved what we should be seeking.

When the Master said, "My peace I give unto you: not as the world giveth,"[2] he was telling us about a state of consciousness which, at this moment, some of us may know nothing about. It is a state of consciousness which our relatives, who have not gone as far on the path as we have, cannot perceive, but which we can perceive, and we may wonder why they are unable to perceive it.

So, too, from where we are at this moment, we may not be able to perceive the nature of the true spiritual consciousness. How many of us can imagine what it means to have arrived at a place where we do not live by bread alone, where the things out here have no significance at all except that they are useful as part of our daily living, but with no concern for what amount is here? How many can imagine what it means to arrive at a state of consciousness that has little or no concern for the digestive or the eliminative apparatus, the muscles, or the brain, but a state of consciousness that has already perceived that these are really governed by every word of truth that is in their consciousness, and therefore the whole concern is to obtain that atmosphere of the Spirit, rather than to attain physical perfection?

Achieve the Conscious Realization of the Presence

What we have been declaring in treatment or meditation, now we are actually expected to believe. Just as the beginner in metaphysics says, "I am not sick: I am well," and does not believe it, but eventually does come to the point where he understands what he is saying and why, so we have been reading in Infinite Way writings and hearing on the tapes from the beginning of this work that the object of the Infinite Way is not to change humanhood. But we have not been able to believe it. Now, after all these years, we are being asked to believe that the object of our work really is not to change humanhood. The object of our work is not to make sick people well or poor people abundant. Our function now is actually to come into a state of consciousness where we can truthfully say that there is only one goal: attaining that "mind. . . which was also in Christ Jesus,"[3] or abiding in that Spirit which "raised up Jesus from the dead. . . [and] shall also quicken your mortal bodies."[4]

"Where the Spirit of the Lord is, there is liberty"[5] must be taken as a sort of shibboleth from now on, a password, so that regardless of what problem confronts us or those who come to us for help, we instantly remember, "Where the Spirit of the Lord is, there is liberty," and do not seek to make the particular demonstration, do not seek to get rid of the specific disease, lack, or sin, but learn to drop those with "No, I must attain that spirit of the Lord, for where It is, there liberty will be found."

This brings us to the nature of treatment or contemplative healing meditations in the Infinite Way. We have no concern with the name or nature of a problem. Whether it is physical, mental, moral, or financial, it is all the same. We are not trying to do anything to the problem. All we are going to do is to bring ourselves to the consciousness of the spirit of the Lord, the realization of God's presence because, when we attain that, liberty and freedom from all discord for ourselves and for those who are attuned to our consciousness will be found.

From this day onward, we have no demonstration to make except one, and that is to bring to conscious experience the realization of the presence of God, of the spirit of the Lord. That is our only demonstration; that is our only function; that is our only excuse for living. We may sit down with the Bible or with a book, read a few lines or a few pages and then sit down and meditate, and come quickly into that response which assures us God is on the field. After that, our work for that moment is finished. We can go about our business. There will be problems in our experience and in the experience of those who come to us which will compel us to do that a hundred times over before that liberty is achieved. The reason is that there are seeming obstructions in your consciousness and mine, and in the consciousness of those who come to us. We still talk beautiful truths, but we have not attained the consciousness of that which we are seeking.

A Transition from Clichés to Living Truth

In and of itself, all of the truth that is written will never heal a headache. But if we can sit down and attain the consciousness of one statement, we can heal not only the world, but raise the dead, if all of the circumstances are propitious. In the mind of the student or patient, however, there is usually only the thought of getting well. Perhaps he has come to the place where the doctors have no cure, so he turns to God, and in his moment of need he actually believes that he wants God. But let us not be fooled by that. He does not really want God: he wants a healing, which he did not get from the doctor, and now he is willing to get the healing from God. God is usually the last recourse.

So it is that even while patients and students are professing to us, and sometimes to themselves, that they are really seeking God and spiritual living, they are just all agog to get well, so that they can get back to their human way of living again and have more of it. That sometimes acts as a barrier to their healing. Healings usually take place when a real, sincere desire comes within to find God, to attain spiritual consciousness. Healings come quickly then.

To some extent, we are all immersed in material sense—some more, some less. The very degree of that material sense is the degree of the barrier that is likely to separate us from our healing. There is no reason for criticism, judgment, or condemnation because of that, for the simple reason that it is not our fault. Remember, we were all born into a material state of consciousness. We not only were born into it, but all our education has been directed along that line.

It is common knowledge that Americans are go-getters, and by now it is a legend how they have come from rags to riches, how they raise their voices in hurrahs for the red, white, and blue. Very often, to experience spiritual healing, we have to reach the place where we lose some of our red, white, and blueness, and decide that we belong more to the household of God than we do to any separate land, race, religion, cult, climate, or creed. When we come to that awareness, we are entering the spiritual consciousness that understands that there is neither Jew nor Greek; there is neither bond nor free: we are all one in Christ.

By paying lip service to that sense of freedom and equality, let us not believe that it demonstrates itself that way, because it does not. It demonstrates itself in spiritual harmony only when, in our innermost heart and soul, we come to that place of recognition that just as the life of the blade of grass is the same life as that of an orchid, so the life of the Jew, the life of the Gentile, the life of the Mohammedan, the life of the Hindu is the same life as that of the Christian. In the degree that we recognize that, do we enter spiritual consciousness.

It is easy to pay lip service to the truth that money is not our supply: God is our supply. But in the next breath we watch that bank account or wallet, carefully counting it and eagerly seeking for more to come in, and all the time, metaphysically we are declaring, "Money is not my supply." Do you understand the point I am making?

We are making a transition from the clichés of metaphysics to the actual experience of living the spiritual truth that we read and study. "Man shall not live by bread alone, but by every word that proceedeth out of the mouth of God."[6] This means that at every temptation or suggestion of a lack or limitation in any direction, we have to face that lack or limitation—not ignore it—look right at it, hold up a banner, and realize, "No, 'man shall not live by bread alone, but by every word that proceedeth out of the mouth of God.' Every word of truth in my consciousness is my supply."

The Hebrews found that when they held up the banner of truth and declared that the enemy had only the "arm of flesh,"[7] the enemy began fighting among themselves and destroying each other. Our problems, too, begin fighting among themselves and destroying themselves the moment we learn to hold up the proper banner, the appropriate word of God. As we look at these "Pilates" who claim to have power over us—the diseases, the sins, or the false appetites—and say, "'Thou couldest have no power at all against me, except it were given thee from above.'[8] You have only the 'arm of flesh.' Man shall not live by bread alone, but by every word that proceedeth out of the mouth of God," eventually that state of consciousness demonstrates itself within us and we find that we are in that consciousness where we can enjoy the world, be in it but not of it.

A Mass Mesmeric Sense Binds Us

The message of the Infinite Way is often criticized because of the attention it gives to the nature of error. It is not that the Infinite Way would build up in anyone a fear of error in any form, but it would hold up the nature of error to our view, so that we can look it right in the face, and then say to it, "Ah, ha! I've seen you; I know what you are; and I shall no longer fear you, for now I understand the meaning of God's allness. It means the absolute nothingness of *you,* you appearing as sin, disease, or death."

In our advanced work, such as *"The Thunder of Silence,"*[9] the practitioner's chapter, "The New Horizon,"[10] and in any of the teachings that I have given to practitioners, I have brought forcibly to the attention of our students that behind all the discords of the world is a mass hypnotism, not a hypnotism from one individual to another but a mass mesmeric sense that binds us. It is not a subject that is easily understood. It is difficult to understand how there can exist a mesmerism that binds us of which we are not even aware.

When we are free of that hypnotism we can see the world as it is; and when we are not free of it, we can see it only from a hypnotized standpoint. For instance, in our hypnotized state we have a fear of our body or we have a fear of lack. That is what hypnosis does to one. It makes us think that we live as a body, and so we want nothing to happen to that body for fear it is happening to our life.

The Basis of All Discord

If we were to look out of the door of our house on to the garden, we might be able to see palm fronds on the palm trees that would be brown, dead, and about to fall off. Then when these palm fronds reach a certain stage of their development and do fall off, we might think, "Well, it's a dead leaf—or a dead frond—a dead branch, so it falls off." In the hypnotized state, we might say, "Everything dies, and so will I die." As we see flowers dying, animals dying, people dying all around us, we may become impressed with that sense of the inevitability of death. Can we not understand that is all based on the belief that we are a branch separated from the tree or that our body is what we are. The minute that hypnosis is lifted, none of that is true. If every branch falls off the tree, the life of the tree is still there, and it will be there forever, for the life is not in the tree. The life is God Itself. If we remove the whole tree, the life will still be there, and it will appear as another tree in its due time.

So with us. Once the hypnotism begins to lessen, we perceive that this body is not what we are. We are invisible. This perception changes the body. Years ago doctors told us that about every seven years we have a whole new body. Later, we were told it was every three years, and now it is said that the whole structure of our body changes once a year or once in three years, so that at the end of that period, the body we had before is gone and we have a whole new body.

Literally our bodies have died, but that which constitutes us has raised up a new one. As a matter of fact, it is doing that all the time. The hair grows out and is cut off, and more grows. The nails are cut off, and more grow. The skin sloughs off, and more skin forms. And so it is that the body is continually sloughing off—dying—and being reborn, but you and I go on forever. We have been going on from infancy to our present stage and, with this hypnotic influence of the world removed, we learn that we go on forever even if the whole body were buried or cremated. That will make no difference. We will already have formed a new concept of body. Long before the body has been moved to the mortuary, we will have formed a whole new body, and so our whole fear of death is overcome. We no longer are concerned with what is done to this temple, because in three days we will raise up a new one, and three days can really mean three seconds. Instantly we are renewed.

Gradually we lose this whole mesmerized sense of thinking the body is what we are. We recognize that this we see is the body, not I, and then we no longer care about it beyond keeping it clean and whole.

In our human, mesmerized sense, we are concerned about our dollars, because we think that the number of dollars we have is our supply. As soon as the mesmerism begins to break, we lose our sense of dependence on dollars, realizing, "Why, no, supply is my consciousness. And just as it is forming new hair, new nails, and new skin every minute, it is forming new dollars."

This part of our teaching is not well understood except by those students who have gone far enough to do healing work. They quickly perceive that the patient does not really have a disease, a sin, or a lack, but that he is laboring under hypnosis. Only one thing can break that hypnosis, and that is to learn there is neither good nor evil in this experience. God constitutes this experience. Thus we lose our fear of the evil as well as our desire for the good, the normal, and harmonious, and then the spiritual takes place.

Hypnotism is at the basis of all our ills. From infancy we have been hypnotized into accepting certain theories of medicine and various theories of human life—until we have actually believed them. For example, there was a time in my experience a few years ago when the idea of social security was shocking. It was thought to be disgraceful to have such ideas. Everybody should earn his own living and everybody should save enough for his old age. Nobody stopped to think that on the wages being paid nobody could save enough to retire. Yet it was believed that everybody should retire at a certain time, and everybody should save money for that day. Then that particular hypnosis was relieved, and we began to perceive that we were under an obligation to our fellow man and that there should be social security for the benefit of those who never earn enough during their lifetime to be able to stay out of the poorhouse in their old age. A social revolution took place, and now we are less hypnotized by our own affairs and ignorance of our neighbors' affairs. We have come up into the freer atmosphere, which everyone attains in Christ-consciousness, where we take upon ourselves the responsibility for our fellow man and try to provide, in one way or another, for everyone in this universe.

It really was nothing but a hypnotic experience that bound us to our old attitudes and made us unmindful of our fellow man's problems. Only because we have come up into a higher atmosphere of spirituality do we now realize that we must make some provision for those unable to provide for themselves.

Becoming Dehypnotized

The human race is hypnotized into concern for the body and for money. Human beings live in fear of their body and in fear of the dollar or its absence. Only in proportion as we recognize that hypnotism is doing that, do we become free from the mesmerism, and to every such fear respond with, "Well, who said that you had to worry about this body? This body is a wonderful instrument of God. Let it alone, and God will take care of it. Do not be afraid of it. It cannot do anything to you. If a finger drops off, you will still go on, or if your whole body drops off, you will go on and you will form a new one, and a new one, and a new one."

When we become dehypnotized in the area of supply, our response to a lack or an abundance of money is, "Why, dollars, dollars? What is happening here? What is that? A million of them? Is that supply?" No, money cannot spend itself. It has no intelligence. If we left the dollars alone, a million years from now they would still be here. They would not be anybody's supply. It would just be dead metal, dead paper. In order for money to have value, we have to take hold of it and do something with it. So it is that the consciousness we are is the important thing about supply, and not the dollars. When we recognize that, we will be surprised that the dollars come in their own way and in their own time. While we are hypnotized into the belief that those dollars are something, we can become millionaires and be afraid to spend the dollars. There are men with millions of dollars who live in eternal fear of spending any part of their wealth for fear that there would be that much less left. There are others who have nothing laid up "where moth and rust doth corrupt,"[11] but who are able to enjoy and spend and have that which God's grace brings to them.

A universal hypnotism binds us to the physical sense of body, to health, and to supply. Freedom from these means that we have respect for them but we no longer have concern for them. Our concern now is not getting healthy or getting supply: our concern now is abiding at the center of our being, so that we entertain within ourselves the spirit of the Lord, for where that Spirit is, there is freedom.

We have paid lip-service in the past to the myth we are not trying to change sickness into health, but now accept this. Let not our concern be for health. Let not our concern be for supply. Let not our concern be for home or companionship. Let our concern be that at least three times a day we find occasion to sit in quietness, in calmness, in peace, until we feel that surging of the Spirit within us. That is what must be our concern. That must be our demonstration, for "where the spirit of the Lord is, there is liberty," there is freedom from hypnosis, there is freedom from sin, freedom from loneliness, freedom from desire, freedom from fear.

To those who have attained even a little freedom from world-hypnotism, life is a very joyous, beautiful, and complete experience, even though our friends may comment, "You seldom play bridge or golf, and you do not go to the theater very often. I can't see how you are enjoying life." When the hypnotism is broken, however, we will be surprised how much joy, inspiration, happiness, and peace there is in this world, and how much companionship, when we are no longer slaves to its desires or to its needs.

So it is that the trials and tribulations that we have compel us to surrender the human sense of good, the human sense of peace, the peace that the world can give, the health that good bodily organs and functions can give. We surrender that for the higher perception of what life is, when life is lived in God. That is where we are functioning, and that is where the Infinite Way is making a transition from the experience of human peace, human health, human supply to the atmosphere of spiritual living, spiritual enjoyment, spiritual supply.

God is Spirit and Soul, and God is our spirit and our soul. As a beholder, we witness the harmonies of God as they appear in our daily experience. Our mind is really the interpreter of the harmonies of God humanly made manifest. Heretofore, when our mind has been hypnotized with concern for the body and the pocketbook, it could not function to behold God's grace in our human experience, and therefore through our mind we beheld this world as sometimes good and sometimes evil, sometimes up and sometimes down. All those who are hypnotized behold it in that way: some human forms of good today and some human forms of evil tomorrow.

In the degree now that we realize that God is the soul of us and functions through our mind to bring *Its* spiritual grace, our mind is free of its mesmeric sense, and through the mind we now behold this universe as it is. When we awaken we shall see Him as He is: "I shall be satisfied, when I awake, with thy likeness."[12]

Chapter Eleven

Making Your Contact with God

A person may sit for an hour or two in a close communion with God where, although nothing is being said, there is a flow back and forth that can be felt, a going and a coming, an in and an out. This is the spirit of God upon one. That flow may appear sometime later as a healing, a message, a new book, or a new class. It may appear as a call to a new country or a new city. One never knows what is going to happen or what will be the fruitage of such a period of meditation.

All Infinite Way students should have not less than one period of meditation a day when they go to God for no reason whatsoever. They go just for the sake of letting God fill them, letting the peace of communion between their outer self and inner self go on whether it is with or without words, and certainly without a request or a desire of any kind. In this period, the student is being receptive to what God wants which may be entirely foreign to anything the student could possibly think of, ask for, plan, or desire.

Miracles, the Fruitage of Opening Oneself to God

An example of what can happen as the result of a meditation in which one opens himself in an attitude of receptivity was a letter that came to my desk asking me if I would go to South Africa. Such a thought had never entered my mind. There was no reason for a trip of that kind because, as far as I knew, there could not be more than about twenty five Infinite Way students in all of South Africa and it hardly seemed possible or wise to make a trip of 30,000 odd miles and coming to talk to twenty five students, especially twenty five students I did not know and only one of whom had expressed a desire for me to come. So obviously I would not have sat down to pray about South Africa or do mental work about it or give myself a treatment about it. It just never entered my thought.

Every day, however, I make sure that I go to God for no reason under the sun—not for you, not for me, and not for anybody else—just for the joy of sitting in God's presence. Then it is that the contact made with God goes out all over the world and brings a call from South Africa. Another time it came from Toronto, Canada, another time from England, and then Stockholm, Sweden. I never had a desire to go back to traveling, and so I had nothing to do with it. But in that period of silence, God made a contact in South Africa, in England, in Stockholm, and in Canada, and I received a call to go to those places, a call which I obediently followed.

Do you see the principle involved? If I had been planning what I should be doing, my thought would have been that my trip would be complete after Europe and that I would return to Hawaii, sit under the coconut trees, and dangle my feet in that big pond outside my door, the Pacific Ocean. But I didn't outline; I didn't desire anything; and I didn't plan. I merely went to God and let myself be filled every day.

Out of opening myself to God's grace, the call came and a

miracle happened in Capetown and Johannesburg. And it is a miracle for me to think that even though I thought there were twenty five people interested in the Infinite Way in all of South Africa, I found 300 eager, expectant, joyous students. Is it not a miracle especially when I had nothing to do with it, never thought of it, never planned it, never asked God about South Africa, never once took it into meditation? I have witnessed this same thing taking place in Sweden, Holland, England, Scotland, Canada, the United States, and Australia. None of this was the result of a desire on my part, outlining what should be, or going to God for a specific purpose. It was the direct result of communing with God for no reason other than just sitting in His presence.

It is like going to visit your mother, if your mother lives at a distance. On the way somebody might ask, "Where are you going?" And you would answer, "I am going to visit my mother." Then they would immediately ask, "Why?" But is it necessary to have a reason to go to visit your mother? No, you go to be in her company and to give her the pleasure of your company, not with an expectation of gain of any kind.

Conscious Contact with God Appears Outwardly as Form

My attitude when I go to God is that I have no reason to go: I am not going for anything; I can't give God anything; and there isn't anything I want from God because spiritually I have everything that I need. Whatever is necessary appears every day as it is needed. So I have nothing for which to go to God. Therefore, there is only one reason left to go to God and that is because I like God's company. I feel I am in good company when I am with God.

I have developed the habit as many times a day as possible of just sitting in that inner peace with God, with not a word, just sitting there and being very content to be at peace, knowing the Father is in me and I am in the Father and we are one. Then that contact with God appears outwardly as the health of my flesh, as the abundance of my purse, as the harmony of my relationships with persons in the world. Just that communion with God, that conscious oneness with God does it all, without a desire, without asking for a need to be fulfilled, without outlining what I would like or think I need. These periods have to do only with the joy found in an inner communion with God.

The Lord's Prayer Is Often Misunderstood

Many persons have misunderstood the Lord's Prayer. They have taken it out of the context of the Master's teaching. When the Master says, "Give us this day our daily bread,"[1] why should anyone think that he means baker's bread when he definitely said that we are not to take thought for what we shall eat? After telling us that, why should he turn around and pray for something to eat? Furthermore, when he was an hungered, he didn't even pray for something to eat. His attitude was that if it's my time to eat, let the Father take care of it. Get thee behind me, Satan; no miracles, I'll make no demonstration of food. I'll do no praying for food. My heavenly Father knows what things I have need of before I ask.

In another passage, Jesus said, "I am the bread."[2] What do you think he was praying for? Certainly he was not praying for food. He was praying for more awareness of the bread of life, the substance of life, spiritual awareness, spiritual understanding, spiritual illumination, and he had the right to pray for that.

Ask; speak; knock. We have the right to ask, "Father, give me grace for today; give me more understanding today; give me more wisdom; give me more spiritual enlightenment today." As a spiritual child of God, I may be fully illumined, but as Joel Goldsmith I have a long, long way to go before I can say, "God, you can stop giving me illumination." I have received only one grain and there is all the rest of the sand on all the beaches of the world for me to go before I ever get to the place of saying, "Stop, Lord, I have enough." I pray, too, every day: "Give me daily bread." But I don't mean food, I mean more of this light, more illumination, more conscious awareness of God's presence. "Fill me more with the spirit of God. Illumine me." That is what Jesus meant when he said, "Give us this day our daily bread."

Asking God to Forgive for Us

When the Master prayed, "Forgive us our debts, as we forgive our debtors,"[3] it is not likely that he was asking to be forgiven in the way we think of forgiveness. He was probably indicating that we are forgiven as we forgive, and he may have been praying for more grace to be able to give more forgiveness.

Well do I remember an experience when I was called upon to rise above a very disagreeable experience concerning one of the students. The hurt was deep for the moment, and it was bad medicine to have to take. In my meditation when the word came to forgive, I answered, "Oh, Father, that's more than I can do. I just haven't risen that high yet. I cannot be that forgiving in this case. I would like to be. Don't think I wouldn't but I'd be a hypocrite if I were to say I have achieved it. But I will tell you what You had better do, Father. You take over and do the forgiving for me because I don't seem to have the ability." And the Father did. Immediately the weight was lifted off my shoulders, and the assurance came that God's forgiveness was right there where I was. That took all the responsibility away from me.

It is hypocritical to make absolute statements of truth as if we had already demonstrated them. It is true we must forgive seventy times seven, but that doesn't mean that we are always going to find it easy and sometimes we may even find it almost impossible. If we do find it almost impossible, we will be relieved if we turn to the Father: "I would like to forgive this person. I don't seem to be making a good job of it. You take over and do the forgiving for me." Then you will find that it is done. I would not be surprised if the Master, knowing what he was going through and would have to go through, were saying, "Father, teach me to be more forgiving so that I can be forgiven more.

Spiritual Enlightenment Appears as Form

Specific requests to God have nothing to do with requests for material good. They have to do with spiritual development. When we ask to be able to forgive more, it means that we are also asking for a higher degree of spiritual consciousness. We would all like to be in a position where we could instantaneously forgive everything and everybody, but if we are not at that state of consciousness, at least let us pray for grace to be able to forgive or at least let God take over and do the forgiving.

"Ask, and it shall be given unto you; seek, and ye shall find; knock, and it shall be opened unto you."[4] That is absolutely right, but do not ask for "what ye shall eat, or what ye shall drink; nor yet for your body, what ye shall put on,"[5] because we have been told that all these things do the nations of the world seek after: and your heavenly Father knoweth that ye have need of all these things."[6] Human beings who do not know any better seek after things, but not the disciples of the Christ. They seek only the kingdom of God, and the things to eat, drink, and wear are added unto them.

The idea that God is spirit is becoming increasingly universal. If you wish to be in contact with God and receive the things of God, the only things you can receive are spiritual, but those things will interpret themselves to you in the outer forms of food, clothing, and transportation. As you receive spiritual light within, it appears without as what we call material form. It may appear as a more harmonious body; it may appear as new organs and functions of the body; it may appear as money, food, clothing; it may appear as transportation. It may appear as a new business or a new opportunity. It can appear in any material form as long as you do not seek the material form but seek only spiritual grace, the understanding of the spiritual presence and power, the understanding of spiritual law, spiritual supply, spiritual health, spiritual companionship.

God Fulfills Itself as Us in an Individual Way

If every one of us could pray for an understanding of spiritual companionship, we would be such friends to one another that we would never need any other companionship. So, too, if there is any reason for meeting and knowing again our loved ones who have made the transition, it is inevitable. Why? God is fulfillment. God fulfills us with anything and everything that is to be a part of our demonstration throughout eternity, and there is nothing of which we are ever deprived. Therefore, if you are to be a continuing part of my consciousness, not all the forces of heaven or hell could remove you from my consciousness. If you are not to play a part in my consciousness, I could not hold you in my consciousness for five seconds. We are all free in God; we are all free in Christ. As we turn to God for fulfillment, God fulfills us in the way suitable to our individual being.

Somewhere on earth there is a teacher for every person who turns to spiritual wisdom. God will not have a teacher left over with no students, nor one less teacher than is needed in the world. For every teacher there is fulfillment appearing as students. For every student there is fulfillment appearing as a teacher. It does not lie in my wisdom to say who are to be students of my work. That rests with God's wisdom, and God's wisdom leads those to me who are mine, but leads away from me those who are not mine and delivers them wherever and to whomever they can find fulfillment.

So, too, if I pass from your human sight, it does not mean that I am lost to you unless you drop me from your consciousness. If you drop me and say, "Oh, he's dead," then you have dropped me, not God. In the same way, if you are a part of my consciousness and a part of my development and unfoldment, and you pass on, you do not leave my consciousness; you couldn't. God would not leave me forsaken, and, if you are a part of my consciousness, you are going to be there forever and forever whether you move from South Africa to New York, or whether you move from this earth to the next plane of consciousness. Remember that whatever is God's plan for you is fulfilled every minute here and hereafter, and those who are to play a part in your consciousness will be there forever, and you will be with them forever.

Reincarnation and Evolving Consciousness

The ongoingness of life makes reincarnation inevitable. But what that form of reincarnation is is entirely dependent on your understanding and the degree of your unfoldment. If you have advanced far enough in spiritual understanding so that you know that God is individual consciousness, then you will also know that individual consciousness is immortal and eternal. It never dies; it continues forever and forever. Since the nature of consciousness is to appear or manifest as form, it is inevitable that your consciousness will appear as form throughout eternity.

Reincarnation will take whatever form will be intelligible to your level of consciousness. When you were an infant, you had the body of an infant, but you do not have it now. Did you die to get rid of it? Or did you evolve out of it? Obviously you evolved out of it. And then when you were a little child, you had an entirely different body, but you did not die out of the infant body to get that one: you evolved. And then you came to a period of maturity where you functioned as parents—father and mother.

How did you get rid of your child body that could not be a father or mother? Did you die out of it? No, you evolved out of it, and you evolved into the body that could function as a parent.

With this same process, the day must come when you no longer desire or have the capacity to be a parent, because you will have evolved out of that stage. Being a parent and bringing children into this world never was meant to be a permanent stage in anyone's life any more than infancy or childhood was supposed to be a permanent dispensation. So the days of parenthood are a period of years which must be outgrown for the next higher form of unfolding consciousness. That is when you begin to live above the physical sense of body and more in the spiritual sense. That is a completely different form of life. By that time, through "dying" daily, you have "died" to the person who was an infant, a child, or a parent. Now you enter a fuller state of maturity in which your higher spiritual development begins.

Many persons miss that glorious period, wither and die of old age because they are kicking every day against the loss of the capacity to become a parent. They want so much to go back to those days that they try to relive it by being grandparents, but they are not content to be grandparents. They want to be parents of their children's children and very often are a detriment to everybody.

A parent should perform the duties of a parent, and the grandparents should have their function. Their function now, however, should be the higher unfoldment of their spiritual faculties so that they do not age, wither, and die, but rather that they make still another progressive step in consciousness and in body. Spiritually illumined people do not die and wither away. They come to a fulfilled period of ripe mature years, and if or when they pass from this scene, they evolve out of one form into the next. Instead of dying they make a transition. That is reincarnation, the constant incarnating and reincarnating in one form after another which, if we permit it, will be spiritual development and unfoldment instead of a withering away with old age.

Your Life Is the Degree of Awareness of Your Consciousness Externalized

There is no injustice or unfairness when you understand karmic law. If you really understood karmic law you would stay awake for many a night and wrestle with yourself to make sure that you are reborn of the Spirit because some day, when you study karmic law and know what it is, you will find out that your life is your consciousness externalized. Your life is never going to change until your consciousness changes. That is karmic law. You can't be higher than what your state of consciousness is. You will never be lower than what your state of consciousness is.

You have a God-given opportunity any day and every day to increase your spiritual development. You have available today what was not available centuries ago. Then Bibles were written by hand, one manuscript passing to another to be copied. How few there must have been who had access to the Bible in those days when they all had to be handwritten and copied exactly from another manuscript! Today you can get the Bible anywhere you want for spare change. You can buy a whole New Testament for a minimal price, and if you write to a Bible house you can get it for nothing. You can buy the greatest spiritual gems of wisdom for a dollar or more. Today there is no excuse for anyone not to be developing spiritually. There are centers for spiritual unfoldment and fine teachers within easy access. Who takes advantage of them? The few. If people only knew that their demonstration cannot rise higher than their own developed spiritual consciousness, they would make use of the opportunities available.

You cannot progress further in life than the effort you put in to the development of your spiritual consciousness. To attain that end, however, you need spiritual teaching in book form; you need spiritual teachings that you can take in by the ear; and you need meditation, prayer, and communion with God.

Without those, you will remain on the human level of life, always seeking, almost begging for a little life, for a little supply, begging for a little happiness when you could be "joint-heirs with Christ"[7] in God to all the heavenly riches. But nobody is preventing you from such a state of bliss. In fact, everybody seems to be conspiring to provide spiritual literature, spiritual classes, and Bibles. How few take advantage of such golden opportunities!

Karmic law reveals that your life is an externalization, an out-picturing of your developed degree of spiritual awareness. That is the secret of life. You can retrograde from where you are now. All you have to do is to be tempted back into the sensual side of life where you spend more time on cards, dancing, radio, television, or whatever these external forms of escapism may be. If you indulge in them more than would represent a normal balanced form of recreation, you retrograde from wherever you are.

On the other hand, as you desert those outer forms and give more time to the inner development of the soul-faculties, with spiritual reading, spiritual practice, spiritual hearing, meditation, prayer and communion, in that degree do you enrich your consciousness to the point where you have that "mind. . . in you which was also in Christ Jesus."[8] Neither you nor I can have that mind in its fullness at this moment, but it can be achieved in some measure. With faithfulness, that measure can be increased year after year. Furthermore, as a by-product, health of mind, body, purse, and human relationships will be more harmonious in proportion to the development of your awareness of truth. "Ye shall know the truth, and the truth shall make you free."[9]

There is another inspiring statement for pondering in your meditation. "Where the Spirit of the Lord is, there is liberty."[10] Where the spirit of the Lord is! Where is the spirit of the Lord? Where the spirit of the Lord is entertained. Where is that? In the consciousness of an individual who is entertaining the spirit of the Lord.

No Condemnation to Those Who Realize Spiritual Sonship

If you were to study the eighth chapter of Romans, you would find a great miracle in it, one that might surprise you. "There is therefore now no condemnation to them which are in Christ Jesus, who walk not after the flesh, but after the Spirit."[11] Have you ever pondered that? There is no condemnation, but to whom? To those who walk in the realization of their spiritual sonship, those who walk not after the flesh, those who do not cater, concern, or worry themselves about what they shall eat, drink, or be clothed, but who concern themselves principally with walking after the Spirit, investigating the Spirit, studying the Spirit.

Becoming Spiritually Minded

"For they that are after the flesh do mind the things of the flesh; but they that are after the Spirit the things of the Spirit. For to be carnally minded is death; but to be spiritually minded is life and peace."[12] Isn't that what you come to a spiritual teaching for? For life, health, peace. That is how to get it: to be spiritually minded. Do you want to know how to be spiritually minded? Abide in your spiritual study and you will soon see that you are becoming spiritually minded.

A businessman who had been touched by the Spirit felt he was very unspiritual. He felt that he was just an ordinary human being. One day in reading the Bible, he read, "Lean not unto thine own understanding. In all thy ways acknowledge him, and he shall direct thy paths."[13] The thought came to him that even if he could never be spiritual, at least he could be obedient and acknowledge God in all his ways. So when he got up in the morning, he thanked God that he could wake up and dress. When he ate, he thanked God that God had provided food. When he went to business he thanked God for that activity, and when he got orders for merchandise, he thanked God for that. One day, he was expecting a big order and did not get it, and he said, "Now, how can I thank God? Well, I can thank God that this man had too much intelligence to buy something when he didn't need it."

This man continuously found ways to acknowledge God. One day he discovered that his cigar was bitter; he couldn't smoke it any more, and it was thrown away. Then he found that he couldn't listen to off-color stories any more and he withdrew from them wherever they were being told. All the time he complained that he couldn't be a spiritual man because he was too materially minded. It came as a shock one day when he was told by a great spiritual teacher that she had heard that he was the most spiritual man in the Middle West.

You ask, "How do you get to be spiritually minded?" That man's example is a pattern that can be followed. In some small way, find out how to keep the mind stayed on God, acknowledge God, keep reading spiritual writings, scripture, and do not expect to wake up spiritual tomorrow because it does not come that way. It is an evolutionary process of "dying" daily, but it is one that you cannot postpone for a day. Each day some bit of "dying" must take place, and then one of these fine days you find you are reborn.

You Are in the Flesh When the Outer Is More the Reality Than the Inner

"So then they that are in the flesh cannot please God."[14] That does not mean that because you are alive and in the physical sense of body you cannot please God. It means that if you are in the consciousness where the outer is the reality instead of the inner, you are not in tune with God. When you come to a place where you realize that some of the things of the outer world are necessary parts of this physical sense of life but not the all-important part, you put them in their proper place. You understand that food is necessary; therefore, you eat it and enjoy it, but you do not become gluttonous over it.

You understand that money is a necessary article of exchange, but you do not begin worshiping it or unduly hoarding it or any of that kind of nonsense, but utilize it sensibly and intelligently and if you have some left over, invest it as wisely as you know how. But you do not treat money as if it were a god that had to be hidden away somewhere or as if it were going to save your life sometime, because if money could save one's life, rich people would never die. Money does not save one's life, but I can tell you that spiritual consciousness can save your life.

"But ye are not in the flesh, but in the Spirit, if so be that the Spirit of God dwell in you."[14] That is the whole secret. "Ye are not in the flesh" even though you are here in the body, even though you are still eating food, even though you are still marrying and having children, even though you are still earning money, spending or saving money. You are in the Spirit, if so be that the spirit of God, the consciousness of God, dwell in you. So, as you let the word of God dwell in you through reading it, thinking it, pondering it, meditating on it, you have the spirit of God dwelling in you, and when the spirit of God dwells in you, there is liberty. "Where the spirit of the Lord is, there is liberty," freedom from sin, disease, old age, lack, limitation. The majority of the discords of the world do not come nigh your dwelling place when the spirit of the Lord dwells in you.

You are the only one who can bring the spirit of the Lord to conscious living in you because God actually is within you, whether or not you consciously dwell in the spirit of the Lord. But it is only as you consciously bring It to light through pondering the Word that the spirit of the Lord dwells in you, and all is well.

"Now if any man have not the Spirit of Christ, he is none of his."[15] This brings me to the statement I have so often made, and which many people do not understand, that God is not in the human world. God is not in the world of those who do not have God consciously abiding in them. In Romans that same principle is stated; "If any man have not the spirit of Christ, he is none of his." If you are not living in that Word and letting the Word live in you, if you are not abiding in spiritual literature, in spiritual meditation, be assured you are no part of Christ and Christ is no part of you, and your life is entirely a human one.

Live Consciously in the Realization of the Indwelling Spirit

"But if the Spirit of him that raised up Jesus from the dead dwell in you, he that raised up Christ from the dead shall also quicken your mortal bodies"—this flesh and blood body—"by his Spirit that dwelleth in you."[16] Do you not see what your function is in life? Do you not see why it is that you are spiritual students and what it is that you must do to fulfill yourself in that way? You must consciously live in the realization that the spirit of God dwells in you and that you dwell in the spirit of God. The spirit of God is your substance and supply. The spirit of God is your health and wealth. The spirit of God is the bond of love between you and everyone else, a spiritual love, a pure love, a giving love. That is the only relationship you are permitted. Do you not see that it cannot be achieved except that the spirit of God dwell in you?

Chapter Twelve

Peace on Earth A Christmas Story

One of our students sent me a most beautiful story as a Christmas gift. I can give you the essence of it but not the beauty. It tells of an ancient king who was peaceable, just, merciful and kind. The neighboring king, however, was intent on war and conquest. The peaceable king sent an ambassador to the warlike king seeking peace. In the meantime, however, in order to protect his people, the king made preparations for war. From one end of the nation to the other, factories turned out war materiel. This activity saddened his people, for they well knew the nature of war. Gradually the smiles faded from their faces, and joy went out of their hearts. Seeing this, the king prayed for some means of changing the situation and bringing about peace and harmony to his people and to the nation.

One day the wife of one of his officers came to the king and asked permission to reveal a secret to him. The king agreed, and she whispered in his ear. The secret pleased the king greatly, and he told her to go out and tell this secret to other women in the city. She was to confide this secret to each and every woman and tell each woman to in turn go abroad in the land and impart this great secret to other women. So, from one end of the nation to the other, women traveled, imparting this great secret to all the women, and the secret spread throughout the land. Soon smiles returned to the faces of the people, singing was once more heard in the land, and joy was abroad.

On Christmas day word came from the ambassador that a peace treaty had been signed with the neighboring king. The king issued an edict that all war preparations were to cease and that factories were to return to peacetime products. He quickly learned that this had already been done. For several weeks the factories had been changing over to peacetime products, and this was in part the reason for the merriment in the land.

The officers of the court wanted to know, "What is this great secret that has been given to our women and that has brought about this great effect?" The king replied, "The secret whispered to every woman is this. 'Each and every day retire for a short period of silence and go within yourself. Do not pray to God for anything at all. Just sit there in the silence and find peace within yourself. Feel peace within yourself'."

This was the great secret of the return of joy and gladness and peace with the neighbor and throughout the land.

Finding and Releasing the Inner Peace

Many of you will not find this story strange because you have already realized that you cannot pray to God for peace in the nation or even for peace for yourself. Why? Until we have found peace within ourselves, we cannot give it to our neighbor nor can we receive it from our neighbor.

God has already planted His peace in our souls, in our hearts, in our minds. The "peace of God which passeth all understanding"[1] is established within us, but as humans we have locked it there. We must turn inwardly and find the peace that is within us. We must release the Prince of Peace from within us and let it do its work in the consciousness of all those who at this moment may be ready for the experience and are receptive to it. In our daily meditations we make contact with the peace within us, and it is released. It flows out from us like the dove of peace and spreads its seeds all over this universe.

It is a miracle of grace that one with God is a majority, that two or more gathered together find the entire kingdom of God in the midst of them. It is a miracle of grace that communing with the son of God within us brings forth all that the son of God is to our universe.

This we have experienced in our Sunday mornings here where in the beginning only a few of us began with the idea that "if I meditate with you for fifteen minutes and find peace within myself, if I find that center where the son of God is planted in me, and if I become one with *It,* then this inner peace—that imprisoned splendor—is released into the world and is felt by all my neighbors." You all felt that peace, and as the weeks went by, you felt yourself surrounded by peace. It became easier for you to feel peace within yourself, and that peace in turn spread to your neighbor. The peace that you found in your hearts—the peace that you established with your neighbor here in this room—was released and went through these walls and reached others out in the world and drew them here to experience that same peace.

Peace Reflects Peace

Many years ago this message was given to us. One who is not expressing love cannot draw love to himself. One who is not expressing abundance cannot draw abundance to himself. In other words, love reflects love; peace reflects peace. Only those who have found peace within themselves can draw peace to themselves. Whatever it is that you would have and would share with your family, your neighbor, your community, the world at large, must first be found within yourself. Jesus himself had nothing to give to the world until the Christ in him had been revealed. Until the spirit of the Lord God was upon him, He was not ordained to heal the sick. "The Spirit of the Lord God is upon me,[1] and I am ordained to heal the sick."

Do not look for peace in another person. Do not look for justice in another. Do not look for mercy in another. Do not look for gratitude in another. Let us first recognize our own barrenness before we demand things from others. Then, recognizing our own barrenness, let us leave our neighbor alone until we have found some measure of Christhood within ourselves; then, peace will be evolving from within ourselves to all mankind.

We do not have to moralize to the world. The grace of God does not reach human consciousness by moralizing. We are not called upon to reform the world. We are called upon only to make contact with the spirit of God within us and release it into the world. There is no spiritual or moral value in all of the words that we utter or in all the lessons we teach or preach. The people of this world will not become good instead of bad, or wise instead of ignorant, through sermonizing or moralizing. You cannot teach anyone morals or a spiritual sense. Nothing will change the human race from what it has always been—in a state of slavery, bondage, and mass ignorance—except by understanding the significance of Christmas which is that the seed of God is planted in the consciousness of each and every individual and that we can bring forth their spiritual and moral sense from within them by first releasing it from within ourselves.

In no other way can peace be established on earth except in the way we have demonstrated it in this room.

If I can find the peace of God in me, I will attract to me a little group, and they will find the peace of God which is established within them, and they will draw it forth from others.

In no other way will this be done. Telling people they should be good, or that there should be peace on earth, or that there should be integrity in dealings, accomplishes nothing. If all the sermons that have been made were actually in demonstration today, we would already have the kingdom of God on earth.

One of the very earliest revelations given to me was that it was not necessary for me to pray for anyone or to give treatments to anyone. It was necessary for me to only find my own inner peace. Then the peace, the awareness of harmony and wholeness and completeness that I found became their experience because they had attuned themselves to my consciousness. When the woman who pressed through the throng surrounding Christ Jesus touched the hem of His robe and beseeched Him, "Master, help me!" she immediately came into His consciousness, and the peace that enveloped Him descended upon her. His peace descended upon all those who turned to Him for help.

The healing Christ is the same Christ who is the Prince of Peace within you, the son of God planted within you from the beginning. We raise up this son of God in us through our meditations, through our inner contemplation and communion with that Spirit that is within us. Our greatest value to the world is in our periods of silence, secrecy and sacredness. Let us therefore retire to our homes, to our temples, to our hills and valleys; and let us find His peace within ourselves. Let us become the center through which the grace of God can escape and be an invisible presence that goes before us to "make the crooked places straight,"[3] to prepare mansions.

The Kingdom of God Within You

The kingdom of God is not in holy mountains, or holy temples, or elsewhere. The kingdom of God is within you. In the very beginning, before time was, God planted his kingdom in the midst of you. How then are we to enjoy the kingdom of God? By finding it within ourselves, by making contact with it, by digging and diving. The deeper we dig, the deeper we go into that inner silence, the deeper we go into that inner soul of our being, the greater are the treasures that we bring forth.

Bringing Forth God's Kingdom

I often think of this. When we drill for oil, when we mine silver, gold or diamonds, when we dive for pearls, are we not bringing forth that which God has already planted in the midst of us? We are not responsible for all that is in the soil, in the ocean, and in the air. We have not created this abundance. All we do by drilling, mining, diving is to bring forth that abundance which God has planted in the midst of us. So it is with the spiritual universe.

Until you find the Christ within yourself, you cannot share the Christ with another. Until you find peace within yourself, you cannot share peace with your neighbor nor can you bring it forth from your neighbor. Until you make contact with the kingdom of God within you, you cannot share Its abundance with another.

Individual Responsibility

It is the responsibility of each and every one of us to find the kingdom of God that is within us. When the Master spoke to the people on the shores of Galilee, in the mountains, by the lakes, in the desert, and in the wilderness—wherever two or more were gathered—He spoke to them and always used the words *you* and *ye. You* must forgive seventy times seven, *you* must pray for your enemy. The Master was speaking to his listeners; he was not talking to Pilate or Herod or Caesar. He did not look to *them* for peace. He was looking to *you.* Therefore, *you* must seek the kingdom of God within *you.* If *you* find peace within yourself, peace will envelop all mankind.

When *you* begin to take the responsibility for maintaining your own families in health and in harmony, you will discover that the inner peace and harmony that you find in your moments of meditation will become the health and harmony of your children and other members of your family. You do not demand it of them. You find it within yourself, and then it becomes a law unto them.

THE SIGNIFICANCE OF CHRISTMAS

To fully understand the significance of Christmas, one must understand the nature of God and the function of the son of God.

The Nature of God

What is the nature of God? God is eternal; God is infinite. God is the same yesterday, today and forever. That which is, always has been and always will be. And since you and the Father are one, the infinite nature of God's being is your being. All that the Father hath is established in you: His wisdom, His mind, His glory, His grace, His presence, His being. The very breath of His life is the breath of your life, because "I and the Father are one."[4]

Since God is eternal, since God is from everlasting to everlasting, since what God has done is forever—then the son of God has been in all human consciousness since the very beginning. Mankind has had within his own soul the divine peace and grace of God; therefore, since the very beginning the son of God has been in the midst of every individual ever created. Two thousand years ago when Christ, the son of God, was born was not the beginning. What took place two thousand years ago was the *revelation* of an experience that has been continuous through eternity.

Christmas is the revelation made two thousand years ago that God had planted in every human consciousness from the very beginning the seed that was to evolve as His Son. This seed—a spiritual influence, a spiritual power—which evolves as the son of God has been planted in the consciousness of every single individual ever born into human experience. No one escapes it. No one has ever existed, or exists now, or ever will exist, without this seed having been implanted in his consciousness and which develops as the son of God in you.

This seed that lies buried within us will remain a seed forever without developing or evolving until it receives nourishment. That nourishment is *recognition.* The moment that I look upon you and realize that within you is the son of God, the moment I recognize the son of God in you, I become the food, the sunshine, the rain to that seed in you. Every time that we see an individual and realize—without expressing it, without writing it—"there too is the grace of God, there too is the son of God, the grace of God is within him," then we become a "light unto the world." By recognizing the indwelling Christ in friend and foe, you release the imprisoned splendor.

Therefore, pray for your enemies. Pray for those who despitefully use you. Pray for your enemies by realizing: There too goes the son of God, the seed planted in the midst of them. Your recognition of that seed within him is the very nurturing that it needs to develop into the son of God and to bring it forth.

The Function of the Son of God

The function of the son of God was revealed to us clearly two thousand years ago in the ministry of Jesus Christ when he said, "I am come that [you] might have life, and that [you] might have it more abundantly,"[5] "that ye may have eternal life."[6] The son of God is all of these things, and the son of God is in the midst of you. The son of God was planted within you so that you may have peace, that you may have life more abundant, that you may find within yourself all that the Father hath. "Son, thou art ever with me, and all that I have is thine."[7]

God planted the seed of himself in each of us, the seed that springs forth as the fully developed son of God whose mission it is that we may know fulfillment, that our lives may be fulfilled, that we may show forth the kingdom and the glory of God. That is the secret of the significance of Christmas. The divine reality of you, the son of God in you, the Holy Grail that you are seeking is within your own consciousness. All the sacredness, the eternality, the immortality of the son of God is established within you. When you understand the nature of that which is inherent in you and which awaits your raising up in you for your redemption, your salvation, your functioning as children of God on earth, this is Christmas—this is the Christ mass—when we realize that we are sent forth to show forth all of God's glory!

Tape Recorded Excerpts
Prepared by the Editor

"Every one of us has the spirit of God or the Christ, an *It,* at the center of our being, but we have not come fully into conscious awareness of *It.* In the beginning you may be aware of it periodically, but you cannot continuously live in this awareness. However, the day comes when this withinness, this inner self, is functioning all of the time and you are consciously aware of it. The few occasions when you are not consciously aware of it, you can restore yourself to awareness by deeper meditation because it is there and it is awaiting your recognition.

"First you must start out with the recognition that there is an *It,* a *He* within you. Call it the Father as Jesus did, call it the Christ as Paul did, or call it Immanuel as the Hebrews did. Recognize that this *He* within you is greater than any circumstance or condition in the world. In the beginning you may have no feeling or knowledge of *Its* presence there at all. In that state, you may have to accept the words of our Hebrew masters, our Christian mystics, or our Oriental mystics—all of whom have found it to be true that there is a *He* within you. There are whole passages in Hebrew scripture and in Christian scripture revealing that there is a *He,* a Christ, a Father, a spirit of God within us. Therefore, if you do not experience it at first, at least acknowledge that these men were wise and truthful and that their lives and the lives of their disciples bear witness to this truth. Another proof that this is true is the fact that these teachings have been going on for centuries. The Master never wrote, yet He could say, 'My words shall not pass away.'[1] And they haven't because He knew that there is an inner presence not only in Him but in you, which will perpetuate his words. If you can't experience it at first and if you can't feel it, accept it as truth nevertheless.

"Recognize it or accept it, and then begin a period of daily and hourly acknowledgment. Acknowledge that '*I* in the midst of me was with me since before Abraham was and will be with me until the end of the world.' Acknowledge him in all thy ways. Acknowledge this presence and power. Even when you have no evidence of it, acknowledge it just the same, because it is the promise and the prophecy of the Master. Agree that it is so, even if you have not yet demonstrated it.

"As you persist with this in your meditations, the day will come when you will feel a quickening of the spirit of God in you. You will feel a peace that passeth all understanding. You will know what spiritual rest means. You will know that Christ has awakened in you. Then hour by hour woo Christ, acknowledge Christ, recognize *It,* give *It* credit for its performance, step aside so that *It* can do a little more while you do a little less. The day will come when this presence will be such a living reality that most of the time you will be consciously aware of it. When you are too busy and your consciousness fades, a moment of not-busy-ness will come and *It* will again rest with you. If the busy-ness is too intense and you seem to have lost *It* or become separated from *It,* you will find that deeper meditation will restore *It* to your conscious realization.

"Acknowledge Christ in the midst of you. Then acknowledge Christ in the midst of all individual beings. By acknowledging It, we are never outside the realm of *Its* protection, *Its* love, *Its* care, *Its* guidance, *Its* wisdom, *Its* strength, and *Its* health."

Joel S. Goldsmith, "The Christ, The Presence In You"
1956 Second Steinway Hall Closed Class 2:1.

About the Series

The 1971 through 1981 *Letters* will be published as a series of eleven fine-quality soft cover books. Each book published in the first edition will be offered by Acropolis Books and The Valor Foundation, and can be ordered from either source:

ACROPOLIS BOOKS, INC.
8601 Dunwoody Place
Suite 303
Atlanta, GA 30350-2509
(800) 773-9923
acropolisbooks@mindspring.com

THE VALOR FOUNDATION
1101 Hillcrest Drive
Hollywood, FL 33021
(954) 989-3000
info@valorfoundation.com

Scriptural References and Notes

Chapter One

1. Acts 10:34.
2. Matthew 23:9.
3. Romans 8:38,39.
4. John 14:27.
5. Mark 13:31.
6. Galatians 2:20.
7. Luke 4:18.
8. John 14:10.
9. Isaiah 2:22.
10. Isaiah 45:2.

Chapter Two

1. Galatians 6:7,8.
2. Isaiah 44:8.
3. Isaiah 2:22.
4. I Corinthians 15:31.
5. Ephesians 2:15.
6. II Corinthians 5:17.
7. Matthew 19:17.
8. Matthew 6:13.

Chapter Three

1. John 18:36.
2. Acts 10:34.
3. Exodus 3:5.
4. Psalm 23:4.
5. I Kings 19:12.
6. Deuteronomy 6:4.
7. Romans 8:1.
8. Ephesians 5:14.
9. Ezekiel 18:30,32.
10. John 9:2,3.
11. John 8:11.
12. Luke 12:14.
13. Romans 7:19.
14. Philippians 3:13,14.
15. Luke 23:34.
16. Alfred, Lord Tennyson.
17. Psalm 23:1.
18. I John 3:2.
19. Habakkuk 1:13.
20. Isaiah 1:18.
21. John 16:7.

Chapter Four

1. I John 4:4.
2. Job 23:14.
3. Isaiah 26:3.
4. Proverbs 3:5,6.
5. Isaiah 45:2.
6. Hebrews 5:13.
7. Hebrews 5:14.
8. Psalm 91:1.
9. Psalm 91:10.
10. Exodus 3:14.
11. Matthew 26:39.
12. Matthew 7:14.
13. Matthew 4:19,20.
14. Matthew 5:11,12.
15. Matthew 11:19.
16. Philippians 3:13,14.
17. Matthew 10:34.
18. John 8:32.
19. Mark 5:34.
20. Matthew 8:5-10.

Chapter Five

1. Psalm 23:4.
2. Matthew 15:11.
3. Isaiah 2:22.
4. Psalm 19:1.
5. Matthew 5:23,24.
6. Proverbs 23:7.
7. Ecclesiastes 11:1.
8. John 8:32.
9. John 5:8.
10. Psalm 91:1.
11. I Samuel 3:9.
12. I Samuel 3:9.
13. II Corinthians 12:9.
14. John 14:27.

Chapter Six

1. Kings 19:12.
2. Psalm 91:1.
3. II Chronicles 32:7,8.
4. John 1:11.
5. John 10:27.
6. Isaiah 45:2.

Chapter Seven

1. Luke 10:20.
2. I Corinthians 2:14.
3. II Corinthians 3:17.
4. Job 33:4.
5. Matthew 5:44,46.
6. John 8:11.
7. Matthew 10:39.
8. Romans 14:11.
9. Isaiah 2:22.
10. Luke 17:21.
11. John 17:3.
12. Exodus 20:4,5.

Chapter Eight

1. Matthew 17:21.
2. II Chronicles 32:8.
3. John 8:31.
4. By the author.
5. By the author.
6. John 8:32.
7. Matthew 4:4.
8. II Corinthians 3:17.
9. Mark 4:39.

Chapter Nine

1. I Corinthians 15:31.
2. Matthew 16:25.
3. Isaiah 2:22.
4. John 18:36.
5. Matthew 4:4.
6. I Kings 19:12.
7. Job 23:14.
8. Psalm 138:8.
9. II Corinthians 12:9.
10. John 4:32.
11. John 8:32.
12. Psalm 91:7.
13. John 19:11.
14. Hebrews 13:5.
15. John 6:35.
16. Isaiah 45:2.
17. John 14:6.
18. John 2:19.
19. I Kings 17:12.
20. Matthew 14:17.
21. John 11:25.

Chapter Ten

1. Matthew 4:19.
2. John 14:27.
3. Philippians 2:5.
4. Romans 8:11.
5. II Corinthians 3:17.
6. Matthew 4:4.
7. II Chronicles 32:8.
8. John 19:11.
9. By the author
10. By the author, *The Infinite Way.*
11. Matthew 6:19.
12. Psalm 17:15.

Chapter Eleven

1. Matthew 6:11.
2. John 6:35.
3. Matthew 6:12.
4. Matthew 7:7.
5. Matthew 6:25.
6. Luke 12:30.
7. Romans 8:17.
8. Philippians 2:5.
9. John 8:32.
10. II Corinthians 3:17.
11. Romans 8:1.
12. Romans 8:5,6.
13. Proverbs 3:5,6.
14. Romans 8:8.
15. Romans 8:9.
16. Romans 8:11.

Chapter Twelve

1. Philippians 4:7.
2. Luke 4:18.
3. Isaiah 45:2.
4. John 10:30.
5. John 10:10.
6. I John 5:13.
7. Luke 15:31.
8. Mark 13:31.

Joel S. Goldsmith Tape Recorded Classes Corresponding to the Chapters of this Volume

Tape recordings may be ordered from

THE INFINITE WAY
PO Box 2089, Peoria AZ 85380-2089
Telephone 800-922-3195 Fax 623-412-8766

E-mail: infiniteway@earthlink.net
www.joelgoldsmith.com
Free Catalog Upon Request

Chapter 1: A Message for the New Year
1962-63 Princess Kaiulani Open Class, Tape 1:2.

Chapter 2: Neither Do I Condemn Thee
1955 First Seattle Private Class, Tape 2:1.
1955 First Kailua Study Group, Tape 2:2.
1956 Second Steinway Hall Practitioners' Class, Tape 2:2.

Chapter 3: Letting God Reveal Itself
1955 Capetown Series, Tape 1:2.

Chapter 4: Progressive Unfoldment
1955 Capetown Series, Tape 4:1.

Chapter 5: A Purified Consciousness
1955 Capetown Series, Tape 3:1, 4:1.

Chapter 6: The Discipline of Knowing the Truth
1951 Second Portland Series, Tape 7:1.

Chapter 7: "Where the Spirit of the Lord Is,
There Is Liberty"
1957 Kailua Advanced Class, Tape 1:1.

Chapter 8: God Realized
1957 Kailua Advanced Class, Tape 1:2.

Chapter 9: Starting the Mystical Life
1957 Kailua Advanced Class, Tape 3:1.

Chapter 10: Surrendering the Human Sense of Health,
Supply, and Peace
1957 Kailua Advanced Class, Tape 3:2.

Chapter 11: Making Your Contact with God
1955 Capetown Series, Tape 4:2.

Chapter 12: Peace on Earth
1961 Hawaiian Village Open Class, Tape 7.
1956 Second Steinway Hall Closcd Class,
Tape 2:1.